"Dave Andrews is a Christian community ˅
practitioner of the good news of peace with
the humble, authentic and quiet way he goe
down (or right side up!)."

JARROD SAUL McKENNA—Nonviolent Direct Action Educator, Social Change
Facilitator, Activist Trainer, World Vision, Perth, Australia.

"Dave Andrews is a man whose life reflects consciousness of God. His personal
piety, kindnesses to others and service to the needy are manifestations of
Dave's God-consciousness. Dave's reflections demonstrate that Muslims and
Christians have much to teach to and learn from each other in respect to
navigating a path towards God and living according to God's will."

DR. HALIM RANE—Associate Professor, Griffith University, and Deputy
Director, Griffith Islamic Studies Research Unit (GIRU), Brisbane, Australia.

"Dave Andrews speaks and writes as a committed Christian actively engaged
in the lives of people of all faith traditions, especially those marginalized
by dominant cultures. His book situates Christian-Muslim dialogue not in
abstractions or dogma, but in the practical concerns of people seeking dignity,
respect and fullness of life. I encourage all who are seeking to follow Jesus
beyond the bounds of institutional 'Christianity' to read and discuss this
important book."

WES HOWARD-BROOK—Seattle University, Author of *"Come Out, My People!"*
*God's Call Out of Empire in the Bible and Beyond.*

"Dave Andrews is already known for his positive work with both (Muslim and
Christian) communities. Dave's concern undoubtedly stems from *compassion*,
that which the *Qurān* refers to when it declares: 'After those [messengers]
We sent Jesus the son of Mary: We gave him the Gospel and put *compassion*
and mercy into the hearts of his followers . . .' (57:27). There is no doubt in
my heart that the best way of building bridges of understanding is through
respectful dialogue. Meeting people and allowing for genuine and respectful
engagement helps us to grow and nurture our humanness. Dave's approach
will surely help us get closer to this noble end."

DR. MOHAMAD ABDALLA—Associate Professor, Griffith University, Director,
Griffith Islamic Research Unit (GIRU) and Director, Queensland node of the
National Centre of Excellence for Islamic Studies (NCEIS), Australia.

"Dave Andrews is that rare mix—rigorous intellect, passionate activist,
theologian and artist, theorist and practitioner—committed to real life at the

sharp end. *The Jihad of Jesus* is an essential read for anyone curious about 'the central conflict of our times'—about how two great Abrahamic faiths, rooted in traditions of justice, love and peace, have motivated such violence, wreaking havoc and destruction from ancient Crusades to 9/11, 7/7 and the War on Terror. Dave digs deep into the history, culture, and tradition of Islam and Christianity and the implications of 'the struggle' for both Christian and Muslim are explored in detail, from the global story, right in to your neighborhood. Dave works hard to rebalance distorted perspectives, rediscovering the rudiments of faith and bringing fresh insights [that] bring contrasting traditions and distinctive world-views together, to inspire peace and development. This book [is] highly recommended."

ANDY TURNER—Community worker and Chair of Greenbelt—"Creating Spaces Where Arts, Faith And Justice Collide"—UK.

"I honestly believe (Dave) has the character that we should be embodying— (better than a majority of Muslims)—and I think that's why he has this affect on us (not being Christian). Surely refinement of character only comes with purifying one's understanding of religion. I've always been perceived by some as 'conservative', but throughout his reflections (on the *Bismillah*) I was in awe, because it was as if he was either reading my mind or taking the words off my tongue. May *Allah* grant him eternal happiness. *Ameen*."

RIFFAT GURDEZI—Northside Da'wah Revival, Brisbane Australia.

"Dave Andrews is one of the leading theologians of Gospel nonviolence. He breaks new ground here, calling us to name our history of violence, reclaim the nonviolence of Jesus and join 'his strong but gentle nonviolent struggle.' *The Jihad of Jesus* marks a timely, original contribution to spirituality and peacemaking, well worth our study and sharing with others. Thank you, Dave Andrews!"

REV. JOHN DEAR—Author of *Jesus the Rebel*, *The Nonviolent Life*, *Living Peace*, and *A Persistent Peace*.

"*The Jihad of Jesus* is an engaging book which tackles honestly and courageously some of the thorniest issues around religion and political violence. It translates scholarly works into fluent and moving language, provides a critical history of Christianity and Islam, and encourages a re-reading of the original intentions of these religious traditions which has the potential to inspire many to move away from violence in their moral and political struggles."

DR. ALEXANDRE CHRISTOYANNOPOULOS—Lecturer in Politics and International Relations, Loughborough University, Leicestershire, UK.

"This book pulls no punches. It explains clearly some of the difficult history of violence carried out in the name of Christianity and Islam throughout the centuries. It should be read by all those who want to dedicate themselves to the path of peace."

ANDREW PRATT—Advisor and Coordinator, Inter-faith Work, Blackburn Diocese, and Former Chief Superintendent, National Community Tension Team, UK.

"This is a greatly needed book. If Christians and Muslims could do more struggling together for mutual understanding and for genuine peace, the 'War against Terror' could actually be won. Dave's book is one of the very few books available today that promotes a solution right at the problematic root of the bitter fruit of terrorism and counter-terrorism. This book gives us insight into what types of blindness, ideology and cruelty underpin the clash between the self-righteous overpowering global dominance of the West, and deeply wounded Islamic piety. The West, and Western Christians, must face our own demons and renounce of our global imperialism and violence, and the Islamic world must likewise face the fact that aiding and abetting the one-eyed violent fanaticism of religious extremists simply keeps the cycle of horror going. The common resources for genuine peace are already there, in Christianity and Islam, in the non-violent struggle for justice of the Messiah or *Masih*—known as Jesus to Christians and *Isa* to Muslims. In *The Jihad of Jesus*, Dave Andrews points out how both faiths have entrenched histories of rejecting Jesus/*Isa* as an example of nonviolence whilst perpetrated horrifying violent atrocities in the name of God. Equally, both Christians and Muslims have astonishing exemplars of the kind of the radical, sacrificial, non-violent reconciliation modeled by Jesus/*Isa*. *The Jihad of Jesus* points us away from the ongoing cycle of violence perpetuated in order to gain some illusory 'total victory' over 'the other', and towards reconciliation, collaboration and transformation."

DR. PAUL TYSON—Hon. Assistant Professor, Theology and Religious Studies, University of Nottingham, UK, and author of *Returning to Reality*.

"*The Jihad of Jesus* is not the *jihad* we are used to hearing about!
It has been hard to keep my heart kind while I have been a part of Christian Solidarity Worldwide, advocating for persecuted Christians, usually at the hands of some Moslem group somewhere.
   "The book is very challenging. It speaks to both Christians and Moslems jointly and examines what might be the causes of our frequent enmities, asking whether they are caused by our faiths or by self-centredness. It 'confesses' past sins of both groups, starting with the Christian ones, and then

it offers things we can do together in a determined way to change ourselves and those around us without swords and violence. It is also carefully showing how Jesus' radical teachings give us the blueprint for this Jihad.

I have read this, thought about it, told others about it, and am still thinking about it. I have found this book a real gem, and it has effectively overthrown in me many wrong assumptions I have held about our beliefs. It shows how we, Moslems and Christians, have so often each misread our holy books for purposes of power and greed—perverting the concept of a personal holy spiritual struggle or jihad into a cause for huge scale brutality. And it sets out the many teachings we share about sacrificing ourselves to bring constructive changes in this world by deliberate and active patience, kindness and non-aggression, the true Jihad."

DR. JOHN HERBERT—The Earl of Powis, Member of Christian Solidarity Worldwide, Chirbury, Wales, UK

"*Jihad* is a much abused term but most Muslims know that the greater *Jihad* is not to use force but to use what Gandhi called 'Soul force' to resist temptation and evil. In *The Jihad of Jesus*, Dave Andrews gives us some important and tested observations on the sources of violence and both the reason and the means for resistance, and he does so by drawing on the wisdom of both Muslim and Christian scholarship and experience. Dave Andrews books come from the heart but also from open and hard-working hands: from his own experiments in compassionate resistance to the violence of this age. For purposeful interfaith engagement with the world as it is I very much recommend this book."

DR. KEITH HEBDEN—Editor of *A Pinch of Salt*, author of *Seeking Justice*, Pioneer Minister and 'Seeking Justice' Advisor, Mansfield, UK.

"Dave Andrews delivers a relevant prophetic charge in *The Jihad of Jesus*. In global and local communities caught in increasing destructive cycles of religious and ethnic violence, Dave unmasks oppressive religion that fuels these conflicts. The radical challenge of Jesus' non-violent revolution, embodied in his restorative life, death and resurrection, calls us afresh and offers us a way ahead. *The Jihad of Jesus* is not primarily an academic work, but instead a work of incarnation reflecting Dave's own proven commitment to living the non-violent revolution of Jesus in his own diverse community."

REV. JUSTIN DUCKWORTH—Anglican Bishop of Wellington, New Zealand.

'The premise of the Truth and Reconciliation commissions constructed in war-torn countries is that reconciliation cannot happen unless perpetrators tell the whole truth about their dastardly deeds. In *The Jihad of Jesus*, Dave Andrews tells the whole truth about the religiously motivated violence, which marks the histories of both Muslims and Christians. In so doing, he paves the way for reconciliation to happen. Dave Andrews skillfully draws out of the sacred books of Christians and Muslims their predisposition for peace and lays out an invitation for us to live into that which we profess. In the *Jihad of Jesus* sectarian violence is confronted by the profound value of peace deeply imbedded within the two faiths which more than half the world professes."

SCOTT BESSENECKER—Author of *Overturning Tables: Freeing Missions from the Christian Industrial Complex.*

"Those that read this book will likely find their hearts slowly beginning to despair for the shame of our past as those who have waged war in the name of God. Yet those feelings of shame and despair are necessary if we are to realize the awfulness of the path of violence. As you read on though such despair will begin to diminish and in its place seedlings of hope will rise. As those seedlings are watered through real life examples your passion for justice will be fuelled and courage will be close at hand. If you finish this book and choose to live by its message you will have grasped that the way of *Isa* is the only hope for our world.'

ANDY MATHESON—Author of *In His Image: Understanding And Embracing The Poor* and Director, Oasis International, UK.

"I can think of no book ever written anywhere—scholarly or popular—that so effectively does three things: 1) Recounts the dark side of both Christianity and Islam, 2) Explores the positive potential for peace in Christianity and Islam, and 3) Shows how the teachings of the Christian savior and Muslim prophet, Jesus, can make a difference in today's world. I wish we could buy a copy of this book for every Christian and Muslim young person in the world, not to mention their parents and grandparents."

BRIAN MCLAREN—Prominent Christian Pastor, Activist, and Author of *Why did Jesus, Moses, the Buddha, and Mohammed Cross the Road?*

"This book is awesome! If your group is looking for a book to study, this is the one! It's language is accessible, the length and format digestible, and each historical citations entreats you to find out more. All this, combined with the invitation to examine our own psychology, congealed mental paradigms, and social relationship to power, politics and religion make this a critical read for anyone hoping to do coherent Muslim-Christian interfaith organizing for effective and profound nonviolent social change in the coming years. This book came out of years of intentional conversation with his neighbours; it has brought me closer to mine."

SARAH THOMPSON—Executive Director, Christian Peacemaker Teams, USA

"*The Jihad of Jesus* is a manual for waging *jihad*. And make no mistake; Dave Andrews wants you to wage *jihad*. Not the violent *jihad* of extremists; but a 'strong yet gentle nonviolent struggle'. Dave's model for this is Jesus: the *jihad* of Jesus. Drawing on the teachings of both Christian and Muslim scholars and faith examples from both traditions he presents Jesus as the supreme example of *jihad*. This is challenging stuff. Dave does not shy away from the litany of horror perpetrated in religions name. But just as you want to turn away and scream 'enough!' Dave leads the reader towards a deeply compassionate and nonviolent reading of *jihad*, teachings which are found in the Qur'an as well as the Bible. This is a book that proceeds with that rare combination of care and urgency. With Jesus as his guide Dave argues that the meaning of *jihad* is to transform ourselves into living examples of love and to fight injustice with the tools of nonviolent action. This is the *jihad* that threatens tyrants and empires of all stripes. This is the *jihad* we need."

DR. JASON MACLEOD—Religious Society of Friends, Academic Advisor for the International Center for Nonviolent Conflict, Washington DC, USA.

# The Jihad of Jesus

# The Jihad of Jesus

The Sacred Nonviolent Struggle for Justice

Dave Andrews

WIPF & STOCK · Eugene, Oregon

THE JIHAD OF JESUS
The Sacred Nonviolent Struggle for Justice

Wipf and Stock Publishers
199 W. 8th Ave., Suite 3
Eugene, OR 97401

www.wipfandstock.com

ISBN 13: 978-1-4982-1774-3

*Cataloging-in-Publication data:*

Andrews, Dave

The jihad of Jesus : the sacred nonviolent struggle for justice / Dave Andrews.

xviii + 174 p. ; 23 cm. Includes bibliographical references.

ISBN 13: 978-1-4982-1774-3

1. Jihad. 2. Christianity and other religions—Islam. 3. Islam—Relations—Christianity. 4. Jesus Christ—Islamic interpretations. 5. Nonviolence. 6. Peace—Religious aspects. 7. Dialogue—Religious aspects. I. Title.

BL80.3 A437 2015

Manufactured in the U.S.A.

# Contents

# Foreword

My good friend, Dave, embodies that "Australian soul" which will better facilitate harmonious coexistence and understanding in our multi-religious, multi-cultural society.

Reading *The Jihad Of Jesus* was like walking down memory lane—seven years of patchwork discussions were woven seamlessly together into this beautiful manuscript.

I found it a thoroughly-engaging, thought-provoking, well-researched, critical-but-balanced, fair-yet-courageous piece of work.

Dr. Nora Amath,

Chairperson, AMARAH, Australian Muslim Advocates for the Rights of All Humanity, Board Secretary, Islamic Relief, Australia

Brisbane 2015.

❧

# Preface

I do not write this as an expert. I am not.

I do not write this as a specialist. I am not.

I simply write this as a Christian, in conversation with Muslim friends, seeking to find a way we can struggle for love and justice that is true to the best in our traditions.

I am writing this for Christians who are concerned about the way Jesus has been (mis)represented by well-known crusading combative pastors, like Mark Driscoll.

I am writing this for Muslims who are concerned about the way *jihad* has been (mis)represented by well known militant extremist preachers, like Abubakar Shekau.

And I am writing this for people who subscribe to neither religion, but watch with horror, as Christians and Muslims slaughter one another in the name of God.

For many people *jihad* and Jesus are totally contradictory, mutually exclusive options. You must choose the one or the other. You cannot have both. Given our present situation, Muslims would tend to choose *jihad*, Christians would tend to choose Jesus.

But it is my contention that—rightly understood—you can't have one without the other. In spite of the fact this may seem heresy to Muslims and/ or Christians, I contend you cannot rightly pursue *jihad* without Jesus, or rightly pursue Jesus without *jihad*.

Reza Aslan's book *Zealot* sets forth the case that Jesus was not simply a pious spiritual teacher, but actually a radical messianic activist. Of this there is no doubt. Both Muslims and Christians believe Jesus was the *Masih* or the Messiah. The debate is about what his radical messianic activism meant in the context of his time and what his radical messianic activism means in the context of the violence and counter-violence in our time.

If, as some would argue, Reza Aslan is right, Jesus could be a model for violent *jihad*. But if, as I argue, Ahmad Shawqi is right, Jesus would be a model of nonviolent *jihad*: as

> *Kindness, chivalry and humility were born the day Jesus was born.*
> *No threat, no tyranny, no revenge, no sword, no raids, no bloodshed*
> *did he use to call to the new faith.*[1]

*The Jihad Of Jesus* is the sacred nonviolent struggle for justice.

Dave Andrews, Brisbane 2015.

❦

---

1. Ahmad Shawqi, *Al-Shawqiyyat,* Vol 2. (Cairo, 1930. Beirut: Dar al-'Awah, 1988), 12.

# Acknowledgements

Thanks be to God, for . . .

My dear wife, Ange, with whom I have walked, side by side, all the way.

My dear extensive, extended family of fellow travellers around the world.

My dear Muslim friends, for showing me how we can live together more empathically and compassionately: particularly Halim Nataprawira, Ali Kareemi, Taher Forotan, Homa Forotan, Shaima Khan, Salam el Merebi, Rasha Kisswani, Mohamad Alshurafa, Susan Almaani, Mohamad Abdalla, Nora Amath, and Halim Rane. Any faults in my representation of Muslim perspectives are mine, not theirs.

My dear Christian friends, for assisting me in overcoming the difficulties I had getting these somewhat provocative interfaith reflections out there in the public arena: especially, Brian McLaren, Shane Claiborne, Jonathan Wilson-Hartgrove, Mark van Steenwyk, Wes Howard-Brook, Michael Hardin, Scott Bessenecker, Rob Wendover, Alexandre Christoyannopoulos, Andrew Pratt, Andy Turner, Jason Macleod, and Paul Tyson. Any faults in my representation of Christian perspectives are mine, not theirs.

My dear professional colleagues, for helping produce and promote the book: specifically my current publisher, Wipf and Stock, for issuing the text; my previous publishers, Authentic, Lion, Mosaic and Tafina, for permitting me to use earlier material in this later document; my editor, Robin Parry, for putting the copy in order; and my publicist, Jaki Arthur, for publicizing *The Jihad Of Jesus*.

*Al-ḥamdu lillāh.*

Dave Andrews

# Introduction

## *Jihad*

*Jihad* is an Islamic term referring to a religious duty for Muslims.

In Arabic, the word *jihad* translates as a noun meaning "struggle."

A person engaged in *jihad* is called a *mujahid,* the plural (of which) is *mujahideen.*

There are two commonly accepted meanings of *jihad*: an inner spiritual struggle and an outer physical struggle.

The *"greater jihad"* is the inner struggle by a believer to fulfill his or her religious duties. This non-violent meaning is stressed by both Muslim and non-Muslim religious authors.

The *"lesser jihad"* is the physical struggle against oppressors, including enemies of Islam. This physical struggle can take a violent form or a non-violent form. The proponents of the violent form (of the struggle) translate (or, rather, interpret) *jihad* as *"holy war."*[1]

Since 9/11 exploded, *jihad* has been imprinted on the global consciousness.

1. Morgan, *Essential Islam*, 87.

1

# PART ONE

## The *Jihad* of *Dajjal*

Both Christians and Muslims believe Jesus or *Isa* will return. But before the coming of the *Masih* will come *al-Masīh ad-Dajjāl* whom the Christians call the Anti-Christ. *Dajjāl* is a common Arabic word meaning deceiver. *Al-Masīh ad-Dajjāl*, with the definite article refers to "the deceiving Messiah," an end-times deceiver. Abdullah bin Umar said that the Prophet said:

> I tell you about him something of which no prophet told before me:
> You should know he is one-eyed, and Allah is not one-eyed.[1]

Some say Christianity is the Anti-Christ.[2] and as a Christian, I must confess, that much of what Christianity has become, in terms of its "one-eyed" arrogance and aggression, is the very opposite of what its founder, the strong-but-gentle Christ, was on about. Others, like Maulana Wahiduddin Khan, say that "the one-eyed *Dajjal* will be born in the Muslim community [and] speak the language of the *Qur'an* to become a deceiver of the Muslims." Maulana Wahiduddin Khan sees the *Dajjal* as "an ideological evil (or *fitna*) leading to a movement based on hatred and violence—in the name of Islam."[3] Maybe both are right.

1. Bowker, *Oxford Dictionary of World Religions*, 43.
2. Andrews, *Christi-Anarchy*.
3. Khan, *The Prophet of Peace*, 155.

# 1

## Remembering Our So-Called
## Christian "Holy Wars"

As a Christian I was brought up to believe that the history of Christianity was a history of Christ-like spirituality that shone through the centuries like a light in the darkness. And in spite of Dawkins, Hitchens, and Harris's claims to the contrary, I still believe there can be little doubt that Christianity as a religion has brought much light into our darkness.

The dignity of the individual is based on the Judeo-Christian idea of people being made in the image of God and the concept of equality is based on the Christian belief that all people are loved, equally, by God, regardless of color, class, caste, or creed. Thus, as I have written elsewhere, there have been Christians all through history who have been at the forefront of campaigns for compassion, freedom, justice, and peace, like Telemachus, Nicholas, Patrick, Aiden, Francis, Clare, Menno Simons, George Fox, John Wesley, William Wilberforce, Charles Finney, Sojourner Truth, Florence Nightingale, Henri Dunant, Mary MacKillop, Pandita Ramabai, Toyohiko Kagawa, Albert Luthuli, Helder Camara, Oscar Romero, Clarence Jordan, Martin Luther King Jr, Dorothy Day, Desmond Tutu, Jean Vanier, and Mother Teresa.

But I've come to realize that Christianity as a religion also has a dark side, and that tragically the history of Christianity is as much a litany of cruelty as it is a legacy of charity. It is to that litany of cruelty we need to turn our attention now. In doing so, I will not attempt to present a detailed account, lest we get bogged down in the detail; but, at the risk of being accused of caricature, I will try to sketch, with the briefest of strokes, a rough outline of an historical overview of Christianity that highlights our dark side.[1]

Christians are not alone in waging so-called "Holy Wars." Many Christians, Muslims, and Jews have slaughtered their Abrahamic brothers and sisters, using the violence advocated in the Hebrew Bible to justify their violence. After all, they say, Moses says, "if there is serious injury, you are to take life for life, eye for eye, tooth for tooth, hand for hand, foot for foot, burn for burn, wound for wound, bruise for bruise" (Exod 21:23–24).

Christ often used unforgettable metaphorical language to express his opinions. He once famously cautioned his disciples about making judgments of others by saying:

> Why do you see the speck in your neighbor's eye, but do not notice the plank in your own eye? Or how can you say to your neighbor, "Let me take the speck out of your eye," while the plank is in your own eye? You hypocrite, first take the plank out of your own eye, and then you will see clearly to take the speck out of your neighbor's eye.
> (Matt 7:3–5)

So, as a Christian, I will follow the commandment of Christ and "take the plank out of my own eye" before trying to take the speck out of my Muslim neighbor's eye.

## Councils, Creeds, and Coercion: Circa 100–500 CE

Christianity may have begun as a voluntary nonviolent movement committed to authentic human growth and change. But it wasn't long before it became a fierce reactionary force, which fervently circumscribed personal choice and ferociously suppressed political dissent.

It was during the reign of the Emperor Constantine that Christianity in the Roman Empire started to align itself to the status quo. Constantine saw the Christian religion as a means of uniting a fragmented empire and the church saw the state as a means of securing a favored position for its religion. and so the deal was done.

In return for encouraging the people to obey the authorities, pay taxes, and serve in the army, the clergy were exempt from being tried by

---

1. Ellerbe, *The Dark Side of Christian History*.

secular courts,[2] paying customary taxes,[3] and serving in the regular army themselves.[4]

And, in return for the sign of the cross, and the assurance that "in this sign thou shalt conquer," in 325, at the Council of Nicea, the Emperor Constantine assured unanimous acceptance of the Nicene Creed, as the standard of orthodoxy, by threatening to banish any bishop who disagreed.[5]

During the reigns of the Emperors Theodosius and Honorius that followed, Christianity in general, and the Catholic church in particular, actually managed to become synonymous with the status quo itself.

In 380 Emperor Theodosius passed a decree that stated:

> We shall believe in the single Deity . . . of the Holy Trinity. We command that those persons who follow this rule shall embrace the name of Catholic Christians. The rest, however, . . . who shall sustain the infamy of heretical dogmas, . . . whom we adjudge demented and insane, shall be smitten first by divine vengeance, and secondly by retribution of our own initiative, which we shall assume in accordance with divine judgment.[6]

In 410 Emperor Honorius passed a decree that said:

> Let all who act contrary to the scared laws know that their creeping in their heretical superstition to worship at the most remote oracle is punishable by exile and blood.[7]

By 435 a law was promulgated that threatened any "*heretic*" who was discovered in the empire with death. The English word "*heresy*" comes from the Greek word *hairesis*, which means "choice." So this legislation meant that, from then on, when it came to the matter of religion, the people in the empire had no choice.[8]

---

2. Hillgarth, *The Conversion of Western Europe*, 49.

3. Smith, *The Pearly Gates Syndicate*, 27.

4. Ibid., 28.

5. Nigg, *The Heretics*, 127.

6. Hillgarth, *The Conversion of Western Europe*, 46.

7. Smith, *The Death of Classical Paganism*, 49.

8. Ellerbe, *The Dark Side of Christian History*, 29.

⟆

Pelagius, an Irish monk of "high character," turned up in the city of Rome at the beginning of the fifth century, and took exception to the establishment over this issue of "choice." He asserted that the concept of "choice" was essential to any meaningful notion of virtue or liberty. and he argued that, if there was no place for choice, there was no place for virtue or liberty either. According to Pelagius, "to be able to do good is the vestibule of virtue, and to be able to do evil is the evidence of liberty."[9]

Augustine, the Bishop of Hippo, promptly denounced the ideas of the noble Pelagius as a danger to law and order. He declared that "free will" could very well undermine the foundation on which the empire was built. Later he was to contend that the "use of force" was necessary *to compel* all those people, involved "in heresies and schisms," outside the fold of the "true" faith, "to come in." And, he concluded, adding insult to injury, by saying, so "let them, (that are compelled,) not find fault with being compelled!"[10] Those who persisted in finding fault with "being compelled," like Pelagius, were excommunicated, at Augustine's behest.[11]

From then on all public debate on religious subjects was banned.[12] Over 270,000 ancient documents, collected by Ptolemy Philadelphus, and 700,000 classical scrolls, kept in the Library of Alexandria, which were considered questionable, were burned.[13]

## Emperors, Popes, and Power: Circa 500–1000 CE.

During this period, when the Roman Empire collapsed, and the Holy Roman Empire was created, Christianity continued to increase its power, as the church sought slowly but surely to take control of the state.

The western Roman Empire fell to the Christian Visigoths.[14] and the eastern Roman Empire was hit by a devastating bout of the bubonic plague that killed up to ten thousand people a day, and is thought to have taken one hundred million lives. The church said, the plague was "a punishment

9. Robinson, *Christian Doctrine of Man*, 180.

10. Broadbent, *The Pilgrim Church*, 27.

11. Pagels, *Adam, Eve, and the Serpent*, 125.

12. Ellerbe, *The Dark Side of Christian History*, 28.

13. Graham, *Deceptions and Myths of the Bible*, 444.

14. Ellerbe, *The Dark Side of Christian History*, 41.

from God" because the state had not submitted to their authority.[15] People, both in the Western Roman Empire and in the Eastern Roman Empire, fled to the Catholic church in terror for the protection they promised.[16] and thus church control of the state was assured.[17]

The theory of the "plenitude of power" gave the pope, as Vicar of Christ, power over all earthly authorities, including the emperor.[18] In an era when people believed in the "divine right" of kings, the approval of the pope was paramount, so he was able to appoint, and depose, kings at will.[19]

This was best demonstrated in the celebrated coronation of Charlemagne, whom the pope crowned with great pageantry, in 800, as the undisputed Emperor of the Holy Roman Empire.

As Phillip Schaff explains:

> To depose princes, to absolve subjects from allegiance, to actively foment rebellion, . . . to give away crowns . . . and consecrate armies, . . . to extort by threat of the payment of tribute, to punish dissenters with perpetual imprisonment, or turn them over to the authorities knowing death would be the punishment—these were the high prerogatives actually exercised by the papacy.[20]

Where there is power, there is always profit to be made. and as a result of the prerogatives they exercised, the church prospered.

The church made money by selling franchises on ecclesiastical offices, peddling indulgences for the forgiveness of sins, collecting revenues from compliant imperial rulers, and confiscating disputed property, by force, if necessary.[21] Not surprisingly, during this period, the church managed to amass an enormous amount of capital. At one stage, it actually owned and operated between one-quarter and one-third of the entire land mass of Western Europe—tax-free![22]

---

15. Panati, *Panati's Extraordinary Endings*, 225–28.

16. Ibid., 225–28.

17. Ibid.

18. Ellerbe, *The Dark Side of Christian History*, 62.

19. Ibid., 52.

20. Schaff, *History of the Christian Church*, 775–76.

21. Russell, *A History of Medieval Christianity*, 92.

22. Ibid., 92.

෴

To groups like the Paulicans, the blatant collaboration of church and state, and the obvious abuse of papal and imperial power, for profit, was "an abomination."

The Paulicans, also known as the Bogomils, "Those Who Prayed to God," (from *Bogu*—"to God" and *moliti*—"to pray"), were renowned for their piety.[23]

They were so appalled by the impropriety displayed by the church, in collusion with the state, that they publicly declared that, as far as they were concerned, the established church had completely forfeited any right it may have had to be considered the true church.[24]

The leaders of the established church replied by saying that they, and they alone, had what was called "the power of the keys," that is, possession of the keys to the kingdom of heaven, entrusted to them, through apostolic succession, by St. Peter. If the Bogomils wanted to be saved, then they should submit to the authority of the established church.[25]

But the Bogomils responded by saying that the only "key to the kingdom" that counted was "the key of truth," and that any claim to apostolic authority that wasn't backed up with some apostolic honesty and integrity was a joke. A bad joke at that. and they wanted nothing to do with it.[26]

So The People Who Prayed to God said that from thenceforth people of faith should organize and manage their own autonomous communities of faith, separate from, and independent of, the machinations of the church and the state and their minions.[27]

Soon, peaceful protest communities were springing up all over the place, like mushrooms. The church and state authorities were incensed by this simple but straightforward challenge to their "divine right" to rule. They quickly marshaled the battalions at their command and, in a series of ruthless orchestrated campaigns, crushed the The People Who Prayed to God. Between 842 and 867 about 100,000 Bogomils were systematically slaughtered—beheaded, burned, or drowned.[28]

---

23. Broadbent, *The Pilgrim Church*, 57.

24. Ibid., 43.

25. Ibid., 49.

26. Ibid., 53.

27. Ibid., 53–54.

28. Ibid., 52.

Looking back, Gregory Magistros, who was himself in charge of one such bloody campaign of slaughter, later wrote: "They were given over to the sword, without pity, sparing neither the elderly nor the children, and . . . quite rightly!"[29]

## Crusades, Inquisitions, and Control: Circa 1000–1500 CE

During the Middle Ages, the church continued to strengthen its control by developing its own ecclesiastical judicial system and expanding the scope of canon law to take in, then take over, civil law itself.[30]

The church claimed jurisdiction in all cases in which the church was involved.[31] The church also claimed jurisdiction in all cases where sacraments or oaths were involved.[32] Consequently "there was scarcely a limit to (the church's) intervention; for in medieval society well-nigh everything was connected with a sacrament or depended on an oath."[33]

The church expected complete obedience to its commands. It would tolerate nothing less than total submission to its dictates.

⚘

In 1095 Pope Urban II called for a Crusade, or Holy War, to be led by "Christian knights" who would take up arms and sally forth to fight against the "enemies of Christ."[34] *"Cursed be the man who holds back his sword from shedding blood!"* was the blood-curdling cry of Pope Gregory VII ringing in the ears of the dedicated "Soldier of Christ."[35]

So, away they went. And, over the course of the next two centuries, they threw themselves, body and soul, into the task of killing thousands, if not hundreds of thousands of "heretics" and "heathens."[36]

29. Ibid., 53.
30. Ellerbe, *The Dark Side of Christian History*, 59.
31. Ibid., 62.
32. Ibid., 62.
33. Daniel-Rops, *Cathedral and Crusade*, 241.
34. Ellerbe, *The Dark Side of Christian History*, 64.
35. Daniel-Rops, *Cathedral and Crusade*, 276.
36. Ellerbe, *The Dark Side of Christian History*, 68.

In 1096 the People's Crusade sacked Belgrade, which next to Constantinople, was the greatest non-Catholic Orthodox city in the world.[37] And, in 1204, the Crusaders attacked Constantinople itself—raping, pillaging, and plundering this great Christian city, in the name of Christ, without mercy.[38]

In the meantime, the Crusaders also managed to assault the Holy City of Jerusalem, and slaughter its Jewish and Muslim inhabitants.[39] It was a massacre. Nicetas Choniates, a Byzantine historian, wrote at the time, with evident distress, that "even the Saracens are merciful . . . compared with these men who bear the Cross of Christ on their shoulders."[40] But Raymond of Aguilers enthusiastically eulogized the massacre as "a just and marvelous judgment of God."

> Wonderful things were to be seen. Numbers of Saracens were beheaded. . . . Others were shot with arrows, or forced to jump from towers; others were tortured for several days, then burned with flames. In the streets were seen piles of heads and hands and feet. One rode about everywhere amid the corpses of men and horses. In the Temple of Solomon, the horses waded in blood up to their knees, nay, up to their bridle. It was a just and marvelous judgment of God, that this place should be filled with the blood of unbelievers.[41]

In 1231 Pope Gregory IX officially established the Inquisition as an independent tribunal, responsible only to the pope, to inquire into any cases where acquiescence to prescribed views was suspect.[42]

The Inquisition was the "tribunal from hell." The Inquisitor was selected not for his equanimity in judging a case, but for his enthusiasm in prosecuting a case. However, he acted as both prosecutor and judge.[43]

37. Daniel-Rops, *Cathedral and Crusade*, 439–41.

38. Russell, *A History of Medieval Christianity*, 159–60.

39. Ellerbe, *The Dark Side of Christian History*, 65.

40. Martin, *Decline and Fall of the Roman Church*, 134.

41. Haught, *Holy Horrors*, 25–26.

42. Daniel-Rops, *Cathedral and Crusade*, 547.

43. Lea, *The Inquisition of The Middle Ages*, 177.

The Inquisitor and his assistants were permitted to carry arms. And, he was granted the right, to absolve his assistants from any acts of violence, committed in pursuing the prosecution of a case.[44]

In the Inquisition the common law right "to be presumed innocent, until proven guilty," was set aside by the canon law order, to be "presumed guilty, until proven innocent."[45]

Names of witnesses against the accused were kept secret.[46] Horrific torture was officially approved, and frequently used, to ruthlessly extract a confession of guilt from the badly beaten accused.[47]

The Inquisition used every conceivable means to inflict unbearable pain on their prey from dislocating limbs to dismembering bodies.[48] Some victims were tied up in ropes, immersed in water, and slowly drowned. Other victims were covered in lard, set over a fire, and slowly roasted.[49] Another torture involved throwing a victim into a pit full of snakes. "One particularly gruesome torture involved turning a large dish full of mice upside down on the victim's stomach. A fire was then lit on top of the dish causing the mice to panic and burrow into the stomach."[50]

One way or another, in the end, nearly everyone confessed. And so those thought by the Inquisitor to be guilty were judged by the Inquisition to be so. The sentences that ensued were merciless.

In 1244 the Council of Narbonne ordered that "in the sentencing of heretics, no husband should be spared because of his wife, nor wife because of her husband, nor parent because of helpless children, and no sentence mitigated because of sickness or old age."[51]

All sentences included a mandatory flagellation, or flogging.[52] A common sentence was perpetual imprisonment, on a diet of bread and water, often in chains, and occasionally in solitary confinement.[53]

---

44. Ibid., 174.

45. Robbins, *The Encyclopaedia of Witchcraft and Demonology*, 13.

46. Lea, *The Inquisition of the Middle Ages*, 214.

47. Plaidy, *The Spanish Inquisition*, 139.

48. Ellerbe, *The Dark Side of Christian History*, 83.

49. Coulton, *Inquisition and Liberty*, 155.

50. Ellerbe, *The Dark Side of Christian History*, 83.

51. Ibid., 81–82.

52. Ibid., 82.

53. Lea, *The Inquisition of the Middle Ages*, 233–36.

Then there was the stake. According to papal statutes, all unrepentant heretics had to be burnt at the stake alive.[54] To his endless shame the hopelessly misnamed pope Innocent III publicly proclaimed that "anyone who attempted to construe a personal view . . . which conflicted with church dogma, must be burned without pity!"[55]

## Worldwide Evangelization, Genocide, and Witch Hunts: Circa 1500–2000 CE

In the last five centuries Christianity has spread worldwide. During the sixteenth and seventeenth centuries, through the period of the Reformation and the Counter-Reformation, there was an enormous upsurge of renewed energy and enthusiasm for evangelization.[56] By the middle of the eighteenth century Christianity had spread to all five continents, and it was more widely spread than any other religion had ever been.[57] By the middle of the twentieth century Christianity was still spreading. And, it now not only had more territory, it also had more adherents and was more influential in world affairs than any other religion in the world.[58]

Unfortunately, that influence included instances of continued church collaboration with the state, utter disregard for human rights, total destruction of tribal cultures, and a direct and indirect involvement in genocide.

One famous Reformer, called Martin Luther, advocated personal salvation for all people, but, at the same time, supported the princes, who were his patrons, in their brutal suppression of the peasants, in the Peasants Revolt, when they tried to stand up for themselves and fight for some basic human rights![59]

Another famous Protestant, called John Calvin, insisted on his right to oppose Catholicism, but, at the same time, like the Catholics he opposed,

---

54. Nigg, *The Heretics*, 220.

55. Tompkins, "Symbols of Heresy," 57.

56. Latourette, *A History of Christianity*, 689.

57. Ibid., 923.

58. Ibid., 924.

59. Stupperich, "Martin Luther," 363.

he sought to impose his views on other people in the city where he lived—by force—even to the point of having his opponents burnt at the stake![60]

One notorious English Puritan leader, Oliver Cromwell, razed the ancient city of Drogheda to the ground, slaughtered its "papist" Irish inhabitants, and rejoiced in the "righteous judgment of God" he had been able to bring "upon these barbarous wretches."[61]

❧

Meanwhile Christopher Columbus landed in America, which he mistakenly took for India, and set about trying "to convert the heathen Indians to our Holy Faith."[62] While Columbus went about "converting the Indians" he set all male "Indians" over the age of fourteen to work, panning the rivers for gold for him. The quotas that were set were too high and nigh on impossible to reach. But those who did not reach them were accused of laziness, or, worse still, theft, and had their hands cut off. When the "Indians" threatened to revolt because of their treatment, Columbus used their threats as an excuse to enslave them.[63]

Conquistadors like Hernando Cortes and Francisco Pizarro decided to follow in the "glorious" footsteps of Christopher Columbus. Cortes made his way to Tenochtitlan, the capital city of the Aztec Empire, in Mexico, where, to begin with, he was greeted with great acclaim as their god, Quetzalcoatl. He used the opportunity to capture their emperor, Montezuma, and keep him as a hostage, so as to control the Aztec Empire. When the people rebelled, Cortes killed Montezuma, destroyed Tenochtitlan, annexed the Aztec Empire, and, eventually, the whole of Mexico.[64]

Once the people were subdued, Peter of Ghent, one of the early missionaries wrote, that the natives were very easily converted: "I and a brother who was with me in this province of Mexico baptized upwards of 200,000 persons—so many in fact I cannot give an accurate estimate of the number. Often we baptized in a single day 14,000 people."[65]

60. Lindt, "John Calvin," 381.
61. Kreider and Yoder, "Christians and War," 24.
62. Mulligan, "Columbus Saga Sinking Fast."
63. "Columbus." In *World Book*, 210.
64. "Cortes." In *World Book*, 368.
65. Neill, *A History of Christian Missions*, 169.

While Cortes made his way to Tenochtitlan, the capital city of the Aztec Empire, in Mexico, Pizarro made his way to Cusco, the capital city of the Inca Empire, in Peru.

Unlike Cortes, Pizarro wasn't greeted like a god. But, with a small contingent of men, Pizarro, like Cortes, was still able to capture the Emperor Atahuapa and keep him as a hostage so as to control the Inca Empire. In spite of paying a vast ransom, rumored to have included at least "one room full of gold and two rooms full of silver," Atahuapa, like Montezuma, was killed, and all Inca opposition, like all Aztec opposition, was crushed.[66]

Again mass conversions quickly followed military conquest.[67] Those "Indians" who did not convert, were burnt at the stake.[68] As the "conversion of the Indians" was considered to be the "chief interest in the enterprise," to most Christians the exploits of Cortes and Pizarro were considered to be an extraordinary success.[69]

It was left to a few, like Bartholemew de Las Casas, a contemporary of Cortes and Pizarro, to lament that "everything we have done to the Indians thus far was tyrannical and wrong!"[70]

It is worth noting, that when the Western missionaries finally did get to India, the Indians didn't fare much better than the Aztecs or the Incas. "Some 3,800 Goans were killed in the evangelization of Goa!"[71]

When it came to my own country, Australia, it was the same old story all over again. Invaders took possession of the land and dispossessed the indigenous population. Those who had the temerity to resist were exterminated, and thousands of Aboriginal people were killed in the process. While some Christians, like John Gribble, did protest the injustice, most did not. In fact, most Christians were more likely to voice their support for the invasion, in which they had a vested interest, and, like John Dunmore Lang, were prepared to go to extraordinary lengths to try to rationalize the injustice that was done *in the name of God*:

> [We] have only carried out the intention of the Creator in coming and settling down in the territory of the natives. God's first command to man was "Be fruitful—multiply and replenish the earth."

66. "Pizarro." In *World Book*, 530.

67. Latourette, *A History of Christianity*, 944.

68. Plaidy, *The Spanish Inquisition*, 165.

69. Latourette, *A History of Christianity*, 944.

70. Neill, *A History of Christian Missions*, 171.

71. Roth, *The Spanish Inquisition*, 221.

> Now that the aborigine has not done and therefore it was no fault in taking the land of which they were previously possessors.[72]

And so the Christian road show rolled on, crushing anyone that happened to get in the road along the way.

❧

At the same time as Christianity was extending its control, it also was tightening its control around the world by conducting "witch hunts" where ever it went.

Pope John XXII had officially sanctioned witch hunts when he authorized the persecution of witchcraft.[73] Witchcraft was held to be the cause behind all sorts of calamities. The obvious solution to a problem was to find the witch responsible.

Once accused of witchcraft it was virtually impossible to escape conviction. Ordinary warts, freckles, and birthmarks were all considered proof of extraordinary perversity.[74] A physician working in prisons where women accused of witchcraft were kept, said "they were driven mad by frequent torture . . . kept in prolonged squalor and darkness of their dungeons . . . and constantly dragged out to undergo atrocious torment."[75] A dissident priest said at the time that the "wretched creatures are compelled by the severity of the torture to confess to things they have never done, and so, by cruel butchery, innocent lives are taken."[76]

From the terrible Basque witch hunt in Old World Catalonia, to the sensational Salem witch hunts in New World Massachusetts, countless innocent people were killed in witch hunts around the world.[77] The Scripture text most quoted by most eager witch hunters was: "Rebellion is as the sin of witchcraft!" (1 Sam 15:23).[78] So, lest they be accused of "rebellion," the "sin of witchcraft," people made sure that they did their very best to be compliant, and to avoid any appearance of disputation with the authorities altogether.

72. Barraclough, *Land Rights*, 2–3.

73. Russell, *A History of Medieval Christianity*, 173.

74. Nigg, *The Heretics*, 281.

75. Walker, *The Woman's Dictionary of Myths and Secrets*, 1004.

76. Thomas, *Religion and the Decline of Magic*, 278.

77. Ellerbe, *The Dark Side of Christian History*, 127.

78. Levack, *The Witch-Hunt in Early Modern Europe*, 105.

Thus, witch hunts proved to be, as one contemporary witness wryly observed, a very potent mechanism of effective political control: "Preachers do not dare preach, and those who preach do not dare to touch on contentious matters, for their lives are in the mouths of ignoramuses, and nobody is without a policeman."[79]

Rossell Hope Robbins called this "shocking nightmare" of total suppression—caused by the witch hunts that were prosecuted over a period of three hundred years, from the fifteenth century, right through to the eighteenth century—"the foulest crime and deepest shame of western civilization."[80]

But worse was yet to come . . .

❧

In the middle of the twentieth century six million Jewish men, women, and children were systematically tagged with yellow stars, then dragged out, beaten up, and shot, or rounded up like animals, thrown onto cattle trucks, and herded into concentration camps, where the "productive" were put to work in slave battalions, and the "unproductive" put to death in gas chambers. "It was the worst single atrocity that our world has ever known."[81]

Daniel Jonah Goldhagen, in his much lauded but most disturbing book on the Holocaust, aptly entitled *Hitler's Willing Executioners*, writes that:

> Jewish survivors report with virtual unanimity German cruelties right until the very end. They leave no doubt that the Germans were seething in hatred for their victims. The Germans were not emotionally neutral executers of superior orders, or cognitively neutral bureaucrats indifferent to the nature of their deeds. The Germans chose to act as they did with no effectual supervision, guided only by their comprehension of the world, by their own notions of justice.[82]

The question of course is—why? Why did the Germans hate the Jews so much? Why did something as obviously wrong as slaughtering six million Jews seem the right thing for them to do at the time?

79. Kamen, *Inquisition and Society in Spain*, 164.

80. Robbins, *The Encyclopaedia of Witchcraft and Demonology*, 3.

81. Ibid., 241–42.

82. Goldhagen, *Hitler's Willing Executioners*, 369.

This is the question Goldhagen seeks to answer. His conclusion is simply this: "that 'ordinary Germans' were animated by anti-Semitism," by "a particular type of anti-Semitism," what he refers to as "eliminationist anti-Semitism" that led them to conclude "that the Jews *ought to die*."[83] Goldhagen then cites not Hitler, not the Nazis, not the SS storm-troopers, but Christianity, as *the single most powerful cause for producing endemic antisemitism in the Christian world*."[84]

To start with, he says, Christians saw Jews as "Christ-killers" and "Christians conceived of their religion as superseding Judaism. Therefore Jews, as Jews, ought to disappear from the earth."[85] Then Martin Luther, the great Reformer who laid the spiritual foundations of the modern German state, turned out to be the "greatest antisemite of his time."[86] "Never once," he says, "did any German Bishop, Catholic or Protestant, speak out publicly on behalf of the Jews, as did the French Archbishop of Toulouse."[87] Instead both Bishop Dibelius and Bishop Sasse publicly expressed a hope of a "solution to the Jewish problem" that augmented the Nazi propaganda program, saying, that they simply "wished them [that is, the Jews] to die out."[88] Thus, Goldberg says, "the church became a compliant helper of Nazi Jewish Policy."[89]

Looking back on the Holocaust in a lecture he gave in March 1946, Pastor Martin Niemöller foreshadowed Goldhagen's findings when he confessed that:

> "Christianity in Germany bears a greater responsibility before God than the Nazis, the SS and the Gestapo. Are not we Christians much more to blame, am I not much more guilty" he asks, "than many who bathed their hands in blood?"[90]

83. Ibid., 14.
84. Ibid., 43.
85. Ibid., 49–50.
86. Ibid., 111.
87. Ibid., 110.
88. Ibid., 108–9, 111.
89. Ibid., 114.
90. Ibid., 114.

One would have hoped that Christians would have learnt something from the salutary lesson of being implicated as *"the single most powerful cause"* of *"the worst single atrocity that the world has ever known."* But I am not so sure that we have learnt anything at all.

At the end of the twentieth century Christians are still actively supporting genocidal policies in the name of Christ. We all know about the part the church has performed in supporting apartheid in South Africa, and the bloodshed in Northern Ireland. But how many of us know about the role that evangelicals have played in Central America, helping dubious brutal government and guerilla groups, regularly cited by Amnesty International for serious ongoing abuses of human rights?

In El Salvador, evangelicals worked directly with the Salvadorean military. "Shoulder to shoulder with the same men who slit throats in the darkness of the night."[91] At one stage the Salvadorean military even made a helicopter available for the Christian Anti-Communist Crusade to drop anti-communist propaganda over villages held by the FMLN (the Farabundo Marti National Liberation Front.)[92]

On one mission Paralife Ministries evangelist, John Steer, toured some eight military bases and spoke to over three and a half thousand military personnel, telling them: "killing for the joy of it was wrong, but killing because it was necessary to fight against an anti-Christ system, communism, was not only right, but the duty of every Christian."[93]

In Nicaragua, evangelicals, like Colonel Oliver North, worked directly for the CIA with the anti-communist contras, transferring millions of dollars in funds from the profits of the sale of arms to Iran to support the contras in their fight against the Sandinistas.[94] At the same time, Pat Robertson, on the "700 Club," a show produced by the Christian Broadcasting Network (CBN), made an appeal for more aid to the contras.[95] CBN contributed three million dollars itself to the Nicaraguan Patriotic Association, an organization connected to the contras.[96]

91. Diamond, *Spiritual Warfare*, 176.
92. Ibid., 176.
93. "Living Words Newsletter." *Paralife Ministries* (September/October, 1986), 8.
94. Diamond, *Spiritual Warfare*, 170.
95. Ibid., 16–17.
96. Ibid., 171.

In Guatemala, evangelicals worked directly with the Guatemalan military. During this period, with the support of evangelicals, the Guatemalan military killed between "three to ten thousand civilians."[97]

In 1976 an American group called Gospel Outreach travelled to Guatemala to do relief work. While they were there they converted a man by the name of Efrain Rios Montt to their cause.[98] In 1982, as a result of a military coup, Rios Montt, an army general, was asked to take power. After consulting with his advisors at Gospel Outreach, Rios Montt accepted the proposal, and so became the first "born again" President of Guatemala.[99]

U.S. evangelicals were ecstatic. In June 1982 Rios Montt's aide met with evangelical leaders to rally some more support for the regime.[100] At one point, a battalion of missionary volunteers and aid of a billion dollars were promised to support "God's miracle in Guatemala."[101]

The first act of the first "born again" President of Guatemala was to suspend the constitution.[102] His next act was to unleash a campaign of genocidal terror against the native population of Guatemala.[103] According to *Garrison Guatemala, "entire Indian villages were erased from the map."*[104] The *Americas Watch,* human rights report records:

> the army does not waste its bullets on women and children. We were repeatedly told of women being raped before being killed, and of children being picked up by the feet and having their heads smashed against walls . . . .[105]

A Pastor of Gospel Outreach's Verbo Church explained the actions of their charge by saying,

> We hold Brother Efrain Rios Montt like King David in the Old Testament. He is the King of the New Testament. The army doesn't

97. Ibid., 166.

98. Ibid., 164.

99. Ibid.

100. Ibid., 165.

101. Ibid.

102. "You Heard It Right: The Dictator Is an Evangelical Christian." *Christianity Today,* April 23, 1982, 33.

103. Diamond, *Spiritual Warfare,* 165.

104. Black, *Garrison Gautemala,* 144.

105. Ibid., 144.

massacre the Indians. It massacres demons, and the Indians are demon possessed. They are communists.[106]

⟡

Then towards the end of the century there was the terrible genocide in Rwanda.

I can remember growing up on stories of the "Great East African Revival," an evangelical renewal movement that swept through Rwanda a generation ago, that Christian pundits at the time predicted would "bring the light of Christ to the dark continent of Africa."

I don't know what effect the "Great East African Revival" had, but I do know that barely a generation later, after the evangelical renewal had come and gone, in early April 1994,

> the country of Rwanda was engulfed in a frenzy of tribal violence, that erupted into the worst case of tribal warfare in Africa's history. . . . Over half of the entire population of Rwanda were forced to flee for their lives! And one million people—men, women, and children—who could neither run—nor hide—were pitilessly put to death![107]

While many Christians—particularly the Quakers and the Seventh Day Adventists—acted heroically, trying to save people who were being attacked, they were themselves hacked to death, along with the neighbors they sought to protect, both Catholics and Protestants had "'key leaders' who, not only 'did not speak out against the killings,' they actually, 'promoted the genocide,' for their own purposes!"[108]

Tokenboh Adeyemo, the Director of the Association of Evangelicals in Africa, says that "homogeneous church growth" resulted in the growth of ethnic churches. And the growth of ethnic churches only served to fan the flame of tribal rivalry, and contribute to the final tribal conflagration![109]

In fact, the most recent research, by John Steward, seems to indicate— much to the shame of the Christian community—that it was "the Muslims

---

106. Diamond, *Spiritual Warfare*, 166.

107. Collins, "Rwanda," 16.

108. Steward, *Rwanda Report*, 1.

109. Adeyemo, "Lessons from Rwanda."

who came out of the genocide 'cleaner' than the Christians! . . . Muslims, unlike the Christians, 'are said to have not participated in the killings!'"[110]

## A New Millennium, the Same Old Story, More Holy Wars: Circa 2000—CE.

On September 11th, 2001, Osama Bin Laden ordered an attack on the twin towers of the World Trade Center at the heart of the American Empire. As the world looked on in astonishment Osama Bin Laden, invoking the name of God, cried *"Here is America struck by God Almighty in one of its vital organs, so that its greatest buildings are destroyed."*[111]

In retaliation, George Bush ordered an attack on Osama Bin Laden in Afghanistan—and also an attack on Saddam Hussein in Iraq (who did not have any weapons of mass destruction, or anything to do with the 9/11 attack, but had tried to kill Bush senior). Reportedly, Bush, a devout born-again, Bible-believing Christian, claimed *"God told me to strike al-Qaeda and I struck them, and then he instructed me to strike at Saddam, which I did."*[112]

The trouble with an eye-for-an-eye policy is that in the end it makes us blind: we are no longer able to see—let alone do—the things that make for peace and love and justice. On the contrary, we wage a one-eyed Holy War of terror against terror. Consequently, we will all remember with horror reports of the allied "Shock and Awe Campaign." Over 100,000 innocent Iraqi civilians have been killed so far, and the number is still counting. Thousands more have lost limbs, an arm or a leg, frequently from unexploded allied cluster bombs, which then became crippling land mines. (The American military has attacked hospitals to prevent them from giving out casualty figures of allied attacks that contradicted official coalition figures.)

Hafitha, Fallujah, Samarra, and Ramadi are names that will live in infamy for the wanton destruction, murder, and assaults upon human beings and human rights.

Numerous homes have been broken into by allied forces, the men taken away, the women humiliated, the children traumatized.

---

110. Steward, *Rwanda Report*, 1.

111. Lincoln, "The Rhetoric of Bush and Bin Laden," *Holy Terrors*. Online: https://mail.google.com/mail/u/0/?shva=1#inbox/14ab542543156511

112. BBC News (October 6, 2005) Online http://www.globalresearch.ca/may-i-quote-you-mr-president/3907

Over 50,000 Iraqis have been imprisoned by US forces since the invasion, but only a tiny portion have been convicted of any crime.

A gulag of prisons run by the US and the new Iraqi government feature a wide variety of torture and degrading abuse leading to breakdown, death, and suicide.[113]

Then there is the associated campaign of "Operation Enduring Freedom" in Afghanistan. Civilians have been killed by drones, crossfire, improvised explosive devices, assassination, bombing, and night raids into houses of suspected insurgents. Up to 20,000 innocent civilians have been killed so far, we're still counting.

The war in Afghanistan continues destroying lives, both due to the war and the war-induced breakdown of public health, security, and infrastructure.

Under-equipped and over-utilized hospitals in Afghanistan are also treating increasing numbers of war wounded, including amputees and burn patients.[114] Hundreds of surrendering Taliban prisoners were asphyxiated en route to prison. And allied troops carried out cruel and inhumane treatment on the prisoners.[115]

Now a coalition is fighting against the so-called Islamic State.

And so it goes on.

113. William Blum, "Great Moments in the History of Imperialism."

114. "Afghan Civilians." In "Costs of War," Watson Institute For International Studies (February 27, 2001) Online: http://costsofwar.org/article/afghan-civilians

115. Ibid.

# 2

## Remembering Our So-Called
## Muslim "Holy Wars"

As a Christian in dialogue with Muslims, I want to be clear from the start that I think Islam, like Christianity, is a religion that has brought much that is holy, holistic, and healthy into our lives.

One of the greatest contributions that Muslims made to our civilization is medicine. In 872 CE in Cairo, Egypt, "the Ahmad ibn Tulun hospital was created and equipped with an elaborate institution and a range of functions." Like other Islamic hospitals that soon followed, "Tulun was a secular institution open to men and women, adults and children, the rich and poor, as well as Muslims and non-Muslims." Tulun was reputedly "the earliest hospital to give care to the mentally ill."[1]

One hundred years after the founding of Tulun, "a surgeon named Al-Zahrawi, often called the 'father of surgery,' wrote an illustrated encyclopedia that would ultimately be used as a guide to European surgeons for the next five hundred years." Al-Zarawhi's surgical instruments, such as scalpels, bone saws, and forceps are still used by modern surgeons. Al-Zahrawi was reportedly "the first surgeon to perform a caesarean operation."[2]

In 859 CE, two Muslim women, Fatima and Miriam al-Firhi, "created the world's first university." The Spanish Muslims of Andalucía were strong advocates of education and helped to dispel the "darkness" that had enveloped Europe during the Dark Ages. Between the eighth and fifteenth

---

1. Craig Considine "Overcoming Historical Amnesia: Muslim Contributions to Civilization." Online: http://www.huffingtonpost.com/craig-considine/overcoming-historical-amnesia_b_4135868.html

2. Ibid.

centuries, "Andalucía was perhaps the world's epicenter for education. Spanish universities such as those in Cordoba, Granada, and Seville, had Christian and Jewish students who learned science from Muslims. Women were also encouraged to study in Muslim Spain." This educational environment that stressed a tolerance that would not reach the "Western world" until the nineteenth and twentieth centuries.[3]

A very significant Muslim contribution to European civilization began in the eighth century, when "Muslim scholars brought the ideas of Socrates, Aristotle and Plato to Europe." Muslims were major contributors to the European Renaissance and the Enlightenment, "two movements that resurrected Greek philosophy and gave new life into a European continent that was bogged down with religious dogma." Two of the most notable Muslim scholars were Al-Ghazali, who developed a reflective "mystical philosophy" in the eleventh and twelfthth centuries, and Ibn Khaldun, widely recognized as "the founder of sociological sciences" in the fourteenth and fifteenth centuries.[4]

And some of the most well-respected philosophers, sociologists, and theologians in the world today include Muslims, such as Tariq Ramadan, Malek Chebel, and Maulana Wahiduddin Khan. However, Islam, like Christianity, also has a side that is not so holy, not so holistic, not so healthy.

I have taken heed of Christ's advice by taking the "plank" out of my own one-eyed view, and focusing on our so-called Christian "Holy Wars" before trying to take the "speck" out of my neighbors' one-eyed views and focusing on their so-called Muslim "Holy Wars." And wherever possible I have drawn on Muslim sources rather than Christian sources of critical reflection.

In taking the plank out of my own eye before taking the speck out of Muslim neighbor's eye I've come to the conclusion that overall, in the conflicts between Christians and Muslims, there have been more devastating wars among Christian states fighting each other than between Christian and Muslim states; and predominantly Christian states have killed more Jews and Muslims than predominantly Muslim states have killed Christians or Jews.[5]

---

3. Ibid.

4. Ibid.

5. "Alive and Kickin'" *New Internationalist* 370, August, 2004. Online: http://newint.org/features/2004/08/01/facts

However, some Muslims have waged "Holy Wars" and still are waging "Holy Wars."

In considering whether a particular war can be accurately designated as a "Holy War" we need to take into account five factors: one, whether religion is a mobilizer; two, whether there is strong support from religious leaders; three, whether religious motivation and communication is invoked by political leaders; four, whether there are attacks on specific significant symbolic religious targets; and five, whether conversion is cited as a goal.

## Campaigns, Massacres, and Enslavement: Circa 620–750 CE

Muhammad was a prophet and a mystic. He was also a political ground-breaker and military trailblazer, like Moses, who used armed forces in order to achieve his goals. Islam may have begun in Medina as a movement of reconciliation between the tribes, dealing with blood-feuds and establishing peaceful alliances with the People of the Book, both Jews and Christians, but it wasn't long before it embarked on a series of fierce military campaigns that included massacres and enslavement of peoples, including Jewish tribes.

In 622, Muhammad led a migration or *hijra* of his first Muslim followers, under threat of persecution from non-Muslim Arabs, from Mecca to Medina. In Medina Muhammad drafted a document for the community of Medina known as the Constitution of Medina, which defined the community or the *umma* in proto-Islamic terms, inaugurating Islam.

In 627 Muhammad martialed the defense of Medina against a siege by a vastly superior Meccan army, in the Battle of the Trench, by digging a ditch that stopped the charges of their cavalry, and sowing discord among the Arab and Jewish tribes aligned against him. In that same year, 627, the Banu Qurayza, a Jewish tribe from Yathrib, who had fought against Muhammad, were defeated and, according to the Sunni *hadith*, all the men (some nine hundred) were beheaded, and all the women and children were enslaved.[6,7]

6. Arafat, W.N. "New Light on the Story of Banu Qurayza and the Jews of Medina," Journal of the Royal Asiatic Society of Great Britain and Ireland, 1976, 100–107.

7. My Muslim colleague, Nora Amath, says, 'This incident is not mentioned in the *Qur'an* at all. It has been disputed by a number of scholars for its inaccuracies. Imam Malik, who is one of the four main jurists in Islamic history, says that the person who told of this story is Ibn Ishaq, who is known to lie on many occasions about other things. Even if there is credibility in this story, it needs to be noted that the judge in

Muhammad died in 632. Under Mohammad's successors, the four "rightly-guided" caliphs, Muslims expanded their political domination through military conquests over Palestine, Syria, Mesopotamia, and Egypt.

> After successfully vanquishing the Middle East and North Africa, in 711, Arab Muslim forces under the Umayyad Caliphate subjugated most of Christian Iberia (present-day Spain and Portugal). Their expansion into north-western Europe was halted in Poitiers France in 732 upon their defeat in battle by the Christianized Franks. But by then they had established a formidable Arab Empire.[8]

However, all was not well in the Empire. In 656, Muhammad's widow, Aisha, led a *Sunni* Muslim force against Ali, Muhammad's son-in-law, whom *Shia* consider to be the first *Shia* Imam, in the Battle of the Camel, at Basra, Iraq. The battle is seen as the first *fitna*—sedition, civic strife, civil war—in the history of Islam, with ten thousand people losing their life in this battle.[9]

Interestingly enough, initially conversion to Islam was neither required nor desired. The Arab Muslim conquerors "did not require the conversion as much as the subordination of non-Muslim peoples." At the end of the Umayyad period, "less than ten per cent of the people in Iran, Iraq, Syria, Egypt, Tunisia, and Spain were Muslim. Only on the Arabian peninsula was the proportion of Muslims among the population higher than this."[10]

However, the Arab Muslim conquest was not experienced by one and all as liberation, for far too many it was an experience of devastation. For example:

> . . . of the first raid into Armenia during the caliphate of 'Uthman, carried out by Salman b. Rabi'a al-Bahili under orders of al-Walid b.' Uqba, the governor of Kufa, it is said: "He went into the land of Armenia killing and taking prisoners and plunder. Then, his hands laden [with plunder] he left and returned to al-Walid."[11]

this case was not Muhammad, but Sad bin Muadh, who the Jewish tribes appointed as their own judge. Bin Muadh judged according to the laws of the Torah. For more analysis and discussion, please see an article by the esteemed Dr Robert Crane, a well-known Muslim scholar http://theamericanmuslim.org/tam.php/features/articles/book-review-the-truth-about-muhammad-founder-of-the-worlds-most-intolerant

8. Pensar, "A Critique of Islamic Jihad."

9. Muir, *The Caliphate*, 261.

10. Lapidus, *A History of Islamic Societies*, 200–201.

11. Yar-Shater, "The Crisis of the Early Caliphate," 9.

## Conquest, Domination, and Conversion: Circa 750–1250 CE

From 749, the Abbasid dynasty was established. The Arab Empire stretched from Spain and Portugal through to the Punjab in India.

> Persians took over the administration with Turks in the army. A dominant military caste evolved with the caliphs providing the regime religious authority. The new capital, Baghdad, symbolized a period of relative peace, prosperity, and cultural progress: the so-called Golden Age of Islam (750–1250).[12]

Even in the so-called Golden Age of Islam there were cases of forced conversion. For instance, in 779, under Abbasid Caliph al-Mahdi, Christian Arabs of the Tannukh tribe were forced to convert to Islam:

> The Mahdi came to Aleppo and the Tannukh who lived in tents round about Aleppo. Then it was said to him, "All these are Christians." And he boiled with anger and compelled them to become Muslims, about five thousand men.[13]

But many Muslim rulers preferred their non-Muslim subjects to stay non-Muslims and tax them rather than convert them. The Umayyads had set up the *dhimmah* to increase taxes from the *dhimmis* (non-Muslim subjects) to benefit the Arab Muslim community financially. "Governors lodged complaints with the caliph when he enacted laws that made conversion easier, depriving the provinces of revenues [from *dhimmis*]."[14]

During the Abbasid period "a shift was made in the political conception from that of a primarily Arab empire to one of a Muslim empire. People of the Book (*Ahl Al-Kitab*)—Christians and Jews—were required to pay a per capita tax (*jizya*) in order to continue existing under the aegis of the "House of Islam" (*Dar al-Islam*).[15] Many Islamic scholars have argued that this tax was a legitimate tax to pay for protection by the state in lieu of military service to the state, but many Christians felt it was a protection racket.[16] "Thus, the only way to prevent the impoverishment of your family

12. Bloom and Blair, "Islam—A Thousand Years of Faith and Power."

13. Budge, *The Chronography of Bar Hebraeus*, 117.

14. Astren, *Karaite Judaism and Historical Understanding*, 33–35.

15. Siebers, *Religion and the Authority of the Past*, 113–15.

16. My Muslim colleague, Nora Amath, says, "This is not how I and other Muslims understand *jizya*. I quote the eminent Sheikh Ali Gomma who is from Al-Azhar, who states: 'When it comes to the concept of *jizyah*, it was not meant to be paid by non-Muslims as sort of punishment for not embracing Islam or a grace conferred on them

was to convert to Islam. Little choice. Other unbelievers (not of the Book) had no choice at all. Convert to Islam or die."[17]

During this period there was increasing Seljuk and Fatimid harassment of Christian pilgrims to the Holy Land. "In 1009 the Fatimid caliph al-Hakim sacked the Christian pilgrimage hospice in Jerusalem and destroyed the Church of The Holy Sepulcher. He persecuted Christians under his rule, destroying 30,000 churches."[18]

European Christians launched a series of nine Crusades over the next 250 years to re-conquer the Holy Land and "liberate" the Holy City of Jerusalem. The famous Sultan Salah ad-Din led the fight back against the Crusaders, whom he defeated and treated with unpredicted and unexpected mercy. But when Sultan Baybars destroyed the last of the Crusader strongholds, he massacred the men and enslaved the women and children.[19]

When Baybars razed Antioch to the ground and killed or captured all its Christian inhabitants, he wrote a letter to its former Christian ruler who was away at the time:

---

for keeping their life intact.' This fact was reiterated by Sir Thomas Arnold in his book *The Call to Islam* in which he states 'This tax was not imposed on the Christians, as some would have us think, as a penalty for their refusal to accept the Muslim faith, but was paid by them in common with the other *dhimmis* or non-Muslim subjects of the states whose religion precluded them from serving in the army, in return for the protection secured for them by the arms of the Musalmans. When the people of Hirah contributed the sum agreed upon, they expressly mentioned that they paid this *Jizyah* on condition that 'the Muslims and their leader protect us from those who would oppress us, whether they be Muslims or others" (Sir Thomas Arnold, *Call To Islam*, 79–81). It was also reported that Khaled ibn al Walid stated in the contract, which he made with some cities near Hira 'if we managed to protect you, then we get the *jizyah* and if we couldn't we don't get it.' When Muslims failed to meet the condition of protection of the people of the *Dhimma*, they returned back the paid *jizyah* to them and this happened during the reign of 'Umar ibn al Khattab when he was informed that Heraclius was preparing a huge army to fight against the Muslims. Due to such circumstances, Abu 'Ubaida, the Muslim military leader at the time, wrote correspondents to all the Muslim rulers of the cities that were opened by Muslims in the Levant area and commanded them to return back the *jizyah* money that was collected from these cities and he wrote to people of *Dhimma* saying, 'we have returned back your money because we were informed of that a huge army was mobilized by the Romans and you placed a condition on us to protect you and we are unable to do it. So we have paid back your money to keep the condition intact along with the contract that was written between us and you and the contract will resume to be effective should we be granted victory.' Online, http://theamericanmuslim.org/tam.php/features/articles/were-christians-forced-to-pay-the-jizyah-to-spare-their-lives."

17. Pensar, "A Critique of Islamic Jihad."

18. Runciman, *A History of The Crusades*, 35.

19. Ibid., 35.

As not a man has escaped to tell thee the tale, we tell it to thee. . . . Hadst thou but seen thy knights trodden under horses' hooves, thy palaces invaded and ransacked for booty, thy ladies bought and sold at four to the dinar! Hadst thou seen any churches demolished, the crosses sawn in sunder, thy garbled gospels hawked about before the sun, then thou wouldst have said: "Would God that I were dust!"[20]

## The Mughal Empire, Oppression and Persecution: Circa 1000–1700 CE

By 715, Umayyad Caliphate forces had started a Muslim campaign to conquer India. Successive waves of invasions followed. Mahmud of Ghazni launched seventeen expeditions and by 1027 the Indian province of Punjab was under Islamic rule.

In 1192 Mu'izz al-Din assembled an army of 120,000 horsemen and advanced to Delhi. Using Delhi as a base he controlled Northern Rajasthan and Northern Ganges-Yamuna Doab, his forces raiding across Northern India as far east as Bengal. "On conquering Varanasi: 'they destroyed one thousand [Hindu] temples and raised [Muslim] mosques on their foundations.'"[21]

Upon the death of Mu'izz al-Din, his general, Qutb-ud-din Aybak declared himself the first Sultan of Delhi.

> The territory under control of the Muslim rulers in Delhi expanded rapidly. By mid-century, Bengal and much of central India was under the Delhi Sultanate. Several Turko-Afghan dynasties ruled from Delhi: the Mamluk (1206–90), the Khalji (1290–1320), the Tughlaq (1320–1414), the Sayyid (1414–51), and the Lodhi (1451–1526). Muslim Kings extended their domains into Southern India. The Kingdom of Vijayanagar resisted until falling to the Deccan Sultanate in 1565.[22]

The Sultanate suffered significantly from the sacking of Delhi in 1398 by Timur, revived briefly under the Lodhi Dynasty, before it was conquered by Babur, in 1526, who went on to found the Mughal Empire that ruled India from the sixteenth to the eighteenth century.

20. Abaza, "Baybars al-Bunduqdari."
21. Sookhdeo, *Global Jihad*, 262.
22. Agnihotri, *Indian History*, 23

Timur's own memoirs on his invasion of India describe in detail the massacre of Hindus:

> "... looting, plundering, and raping of their women and children, their forced conversions to Islam, and the plunder of the wealth of Hindustan." It gives details of "how villages, towns and entire cities were rid of their Hindu male population through systematic mass slaughters and their women and children forcefully converted en masse to Islam."[23]

When Timur attacked the "idolatrous" Hindus he showed them no mercy:

> Before the battle for Delhi, Timur "executed more than one hundred thousand Hindu captives." And when Delhi was captured, "the city was sacked, destroyed, and left in ruins." In his own words, Timur wrote, "Excepting the quarter of the saiyids, the 'ulama and the other Musalmans, the whole city was sacked." And having sacked the city, almost all the survivors were captured and enslaved.[24]

Timur was followed by Babur, who established the mighty Mughal Empire. During Babur's conquests of India "many Hindu temples were destroyed, including the (much loved and still lamented) temple of Ayodha where a mosque was built in its place,"[25] and many Hindu captives were slaughtered: "Those [Hindu captives] who were brought alive [into his camp] were beheaded, after which a tower of skulls was erected in the camp."[26]

Two other famous rulers in the Mughal era were Akbar (c. 1556–1605) and Aurangzeb (c. 1658–1707). Both emperors expanded the empire and were able administrators.

Akbar, who was known for his religious tolerance, and even abolished the *jizya*, was still merciless towards any "infidel" who dared to resist the imposition of his imperial power. In taking the Hindu fortress of Chitor: "at early dawn the Emperor [Akbar] went in mounted on an elephant. The order was given to massacre the infidels as a punishment. . . . By midday 2,000 had been slain."[27]

---

23. Elliot and Dowson, *The History of India*, 389.

24. Ibid., 389.

25. Sookhdeo, *Global Jihad*, 263.

26. Babur, *The Baburnama*, 188.

27. Ahmad, "Tarikh-i-Alfi," 174.

Aurangzeb, was a zealous Muslim and ruthless advocate of a more extremist Islam, reinstituting the *jizya* tax for non-Muslims,[28] and relentlessly harassing the "infidels":

> laying waste the country [in North and Central India], destroying temples, making prisoners of the women and children of the infidels[29] . . . commanding Hindus in the North-West Frontier to convert or be executed, promising those who converted he would cancel all their debts and pardon all their crimes.[30]

## The Ottoman Empire, Aggression and Annihilation: Circa 1000–1920 CE

Many Turkic tribes of Central Asia converted to Islam and became the *ghazis* or warriors in the war against the Byzantine Empire and the establishment of the Seljuk Sultanate. In 1071 the Seljuks won a major battle against the Byzantines at Manzikert, and within a decade the Seljuks conquered Armenia and controlled three-quarters of Asia Minor.[31]

Having gained power, the Seljuks divided their Sultanate into principalities. One of these was the Ottoman dynasty founded by Osman (*Othman* in Arabic). Right from the start it was a *ghazi* Islamic state "dedicated to *Gaza*, the holy war against infidel Christianity."[32]

The Ottomans invited the fierce Muslim *ghazis* to join them in the conquest of Christian countries like Greece, Macedonia, and Bulgaria. In 1389 the Turks conquered the Serbs; in 1453 the Turks captured Constantinople; in 1517 the Turks occupied Syria and Egypt; and in 1529 and 1683 the Turks even extended their empire as far as Austria. And so for 600 years the Ottoman Empire became the most dominant Muslim power in the world.[33]

The Ottomans introduced *surgon* or forced relocation of Turks into the Balkans, Cyprus, Greece, and Serbia, where they were used to control conquered Christian populations.[34] Under Murad I (1360–89), the Otto-

---

28. Elliot and Dowson, *The History of India, vol. 7, 205.*

29. Khan, "Muntakhabu-l Lubab," 300.

30. Sookhdeo, *Global Jihad*, 243.

31. Ibid., 227.

32. Inalcik, *The Ottoman Empire*, 3.

33. Sookhdeo, *Global Jihad*, 231.

34. Ibid., 232.

mans replaced their troops with *kapikkullari* or slave soldiers, and under Murad II (1421–51) replaced them with *janissaries*—Christian boys taken from their families, forced to become Muslims and trained to fight against other Christians.[35]

The capture of Constantinople by the Ottomans and the massacres of noncombatants by the *janissaries* was so calamitous it was never to be forgotten—either by Muslims or Christians.

> "Sultan Mehmed issued an order [that the city be] plundered. From all directions they [the gazis] came. . . . They entered the city, passed the infidels over the sword [i.e. slaughtered them], . . . cut off the head of the emperor and slew the miserable common people. . . . They placed (survivors) in chains, placed metal rings round their necks. . . . According to eyewitnesses, "A great slaughter occurred. . . . (People) fell victim to the violence of the Janissaries. . . . [T]hey killed so as to frighten all the city and terrorize and enslave all by the slaughter. . . . The Turks arrived at the church [the great church of St. Sophia] pillaging, slaughtering, and enslaving. . . . They slew mercilessly all the elderly, both men and women. . . . Newborn infants were thrown into the streets. . . . They enslaved all those who survived. . . . Women and children being led off were tied and bound."
>
> In a letter to the Shah of Iran, Mehmed writes that the inhabitants of the city "have become food for the swords and arrows of the gazis," and those men and women who survived the massacre were thrown into chains. In his letter to the Sultan of Egypt, Mehmed writes, "they killed the pagan inhabitants and destroyed their houses. . . . They cleared these places of their Christian impurity and their monkish filth."[36]

⚬

But as calamitous as the conquest of Constantinople was, it was Armenia that was forced to experience the worst catastrophes of the Turkish "holy war against Christianity."[37]

35. Palmer, "The Origin of Janissarie."

36. Vryonis, "A Critical Analysis of Stanford J. Shaw's *History of the Ottoman Empire and Modern Turkey*," 57–60, 62, 68.

37. Inalcik, *The Ottoman Empire*, 3.

In 640 the initial Muslim attack on Dvin, a major city in Christian Armenia, "put the multitude of the city's population to the sword. Having plundered the city they left . . . leading away the host of captives, 35,000 souls."[38]

In 642–43, the next few waves of attack "spread raids over the entire region with the sword, and took plunder and captives"; took "the fortress of Khram, slaughtered [its garrison] with the sword and took captive the women and children."[39]

In 655 "they ravaged all the lands of Armenia, and stripped all the churches."[40]

From 1048 to 1054 Toghrul Beg "hurled his hordes" at Armenia. His cousin Koutulmish took Ardzen, [and] gave the city [and its 800 churches] over to flames after plundering it and taking from the district 150,000 persons into virtual slavery.[41]

In 1059 Toghrul captured Sivas (a commercial center), reduced it to ruins, and slaughtered the major part of the population. The survivors were carried away into slavery.

In 1064 Alp-Arslan, nephew of Toghrul, "even more cruel than his uncle," attacked the city of Ani. "A frightful butchery followed, blood flowed in torrents, thousands fell by the sword. 'Men were slaughtered in the streets,' says Aristakes Lastivert, 'women carried away, . . . virgins violated in public, . . . infants crushed on the pavements.'"[42]

Between 1894 and 1922 Turkish attacks on the Armenians reached their apotheosis. Turkey decided to "resolve its Armenian [issue] by the destruction of the Armenian race."[43]

According to the Armenian Patriarchate, there were approximately three million Armenians living in the Ottoman Empire in 1878.[44] These Christian Armenians were referred to by Muslim Turks as "*gavours*,

---

38. Sebeos, *The Armenian History Attributed to Sebeos,* 100–101, 246–47.

39. Ibid., 150–51.

40. Ibid., 109

41. Kurkjian, *A History Of Armenia,* 206.

42. Ibid., 206–9.

43. Wolff-Metternich, *German Ambassador to Turkey.* In Hovannisian, *The Armenian Genocide,* xii.

44. Hambaryan, *Hay Zhoghovrdi Patmut'yun 6,* 22.

or infidels."[45] The British ethnographer William Ramsay described the conditions the Armenians endured:

> We must go back to an older time, if we want to appreciate what uncontrolled Turkish rule meant, alike to Armenians and to Greeks. It did not mean religious persecution; it meant unutterable contempt. They were dogs and pigs; and their nature was to be Christians, to be spat upon, if their shadow darkened a Turk, to be outraged, to be the mats on which he wiped the mud from his feet. . . . Nothing that belonged to the Armenian, neither his property, his house, his life, his person, nor his family, was sacred or safe from violence—capricious, unprovoked violence—to resist which by violence meant death![46]

In the late 1870s, "the Greeks, along with several other Christian nations in the Balkans, broke free of Ottoman rule." The Armenians "remained, by and large, passive during these years, earning them the title of *millet-i sadika* or the 'loyal community.'"[47]

The Armenian Communal Council petitioned their Ottoman rulers to deal with: "the looting and murder in Armenian towns by [Muslim] Kurds and Circassians." Nothing was done. Since 1876, the Ottoman ruler had been Sultan Abdul Hamid II. He dismissed the Armenian complaints of looting and murder as largely exaggerated or fabricated.[48] So, after the 1877–78 Russo-Turkish War, with the help of the Russian Empire, the Armenians started to seek greater autonomy and security in the Ottoman Empire.[49]

In 1890, Hamid II created a paramilitary outfit known as the *Hamidiye*, made up of Kurdish irregulars who were tasked to "deal with the Armenians as they wished."[50]

In 1895, 2,000 the Armenians assembled in Constantinople to petition for the reforms they had requested; but "Ottoman police units converged on the rally and violently broke it up."[51] The Hamidian massacres

45. Balakian, *The Burning Tigris*, 25.

46. Ramsay, *Impressions of Turkey*, 206–7.

47. Akcam, *A Shameful Act*, 24.

48. Balakian, *The Burning Tigris*. 445

49. Akcam, *A Shameful Act*, 24.

50. Balakian, *The Burning Tigris*, 445.

51. Ibid., 57–58.

that followed in Bitlis, Diyarbekir, Erzerum, Harput, Sivas, Trabzon *killed between 100,000 and 300,000 Armenians.*[52]

In 1908 officers in the Ottoman Third Army overthrew Hammid II. In the fighting that followed the coup and the counter-coup even more Armenians were massacred in Adana. In the Adana Massacre between 15,000 and 30,000 Armenians were killed.[53]

In 1912 the First Balkan War broke out, the Ottomans were defeated and lost 85 percent of their Empire in Europe. Hundreds of thousands of Muslims, including Circassians and Chechens (known as *muhajirs*), were expelled from the Balkans. And the *muhajirs* were eager to take their revenge against the Christian Armenians.[54]

In 1914 the Ottoman Empire entered World War I on the side of Germany hoping to regain territories lost to Russia after the Russo-Turkish War of 1877–78. However, the Turks were defeated by the Russians, with the help of Armenian volunteer units.[55]

In 1915 The Armenian Holocaust began in earnest. It started with the arrest and execution of some 250 Armenian intellectuals and community leaders in Constantinople,[56] which was then followed by "the wholesale killing of the able-bodied male population through massacre and forced labor, and the deportation of women, children, the elderly and infirm on death marches to the Syrian Desert."[57] The *New York Times* reported that "the roads and the Euphrates are strewn with corpses of exiles, and those who survive are doomed to certain death. It is a plan to exterminate the whole Armenian people."[58]

The United States ambassador wrote,

52. The German Foreign Ministry operative, Ernst Jackh, estimated that 200,000 Armenians were killed and a further 50,000 expelled from the provinces during the Hamidian unrest. French diplomats placed the figures at 250,000 killed. The German pastor Johannes Lepsius was more meticulous in his calculations, counting the deaths of 88,000 Armenians and the destruction of 2,500 villages, 645 churches and monasteries, and the plundering of hundreds of churches, of which 328 were converted into mosques. In Dadrian, *The History of the Armenian Genocide*, 155

53. Akcam, *A Shameful Act*, 69.

54. Ibid., 86–87.

55. Balakian, *The Burning Tigris*, 200.

56. Chisholm, "Constantinople, the Capital of the Turkish Empire."

57. Walker, *Armenia*, 200–203.

58. "Armenians are sent to perish in desert; Turks accused of plan to exterminate whole population; people of Karahissar massacred." *New York Times*, 18 August 1915.

all over the Armenian provinces, in the spring and summer months of 1915, Death in its several forms—massacre, starvation, exhaustion—destroyed the larger part of the refugees. The Turkish policy was that of extermination under the guise of deportation.[59]

Lt. Hasan Maruf, of the Ottoman army, describes how a population of a village were taken all together, and then burned. "The shortest method for disposing of the women and children concentrated in the various camps was to burn them."[60]

Eitan Belkind was a Nili member, who infiltrated the Ottoman army as an official. He was assigned to the headquarters of Kamal Pasha. He claims to have himself witnessed the burning of 5,000 Armenians.[61]

In 2002 I visited the Armenian Genocide Museum in Yerevan with my good friend, Armen Gakavian, whose own family fled the holocaust. There we were reminded that the total number of people killed has been estimated at *between 1 and 1.5 million—half of the entire Armenian population!* [62] Other Christian ethnic groups, such as Assyrians and Greeks, were also killed in the genocide.[63]

## Modern Islamist Radicalism, Extremism and Terrorism: Circa 1920–2020 CE

Both Arabs and Jews invoke strong religious arguments for their ongoing unresolved conflict with regard to the "Promised Land" and the "Chosen City" of Jerusalem.[64] Jews invoke a biblical claim to the Land of Israel.[65]

59. Morgenthau, *Ambassador Morgenthau's Story.*

60. Toynvbee, *British Foreign Office.*

61. Auron, *The Banality of Indifference,* 181–83.

62. Council of Europe Parliamentary Assembly Resolution. "Armenian genocide." Online: http://www.armenian-genocide.org/Affirmation.153/current_category.7/affirmation_detail.html

63. To date, twenty-three countries have officially recognized the events of the period as genocide, and most genocide scholars and historians accept this view. Turkey, the successor state of the Ottoman Empire, denies the word "genocide" as an accurate description of the events. In recent years, Turkish intellectuals have called for Turkey to acknowledge the "Great Catastrophe" and more than 30,000 Turks have called on the Turkish government to apologize to the Armenians, as indeed the Kurds have already done. Based on private correspondence with Dr. Armen Gakavian in 2014.

64. Beker, *The Chosen.*

65. "Likud—Platform." Knesset.gov.il. See, https://web.archive.org/web/2008100

Muslims invoke a *Qur'anic* claim to the Land of Canaan. Contrary to the Jewish claim that this land was promised only to the descendants of Abraham's younger son Isaac, Muslims argue that the Land of Canaan was promised to the elder son, Ishmael, from whom Arabs claim descent.[66]

The PLO (Palestinian Liberation Organization) says in its charter that it is committed to the "liberation of Palestine [that] will destroy the Zionist and imperialist presence."[67] And Hamas, which is now the legitimate government in the Gaza Strip, claims "all of the land of Palestine [that is all the current Israeli and Palestinian territories] is an Islamic *waqf* that must be governed by Muslims."[68]

The conflict between Jews and Arabs in Palestine increased in the twentieth century, erupting into a civil war in 1947, an Arab-Israeli War in 1948, retribution operations from 1951 to 1955, the Suez War in 1956, the Six-Day War in 1967, the War of Attrition from 1967 to 1970, the Yom Kippur War in 1973, the South Lebanon conflict in 1978, the First Lebanon War in 1982, the South Lebanon conflict from 1982 to 2000, the First *Intafada* from 1987 to 1993, the Second *Intafada* from 2000 to 2004, the Second Lebanon War in 2006, the Gaza War from 2008 to 2009, and Operation Pillar of Defense in 2012.

It is estimated that from 1945 to 1995 the conflict took 92,000 lives (74,000 combatants and 18,000 noncombatants).[69] And from 29 September 2000 to 2 October 2012, the conflict took another 7,714 lives.[70] And over all that time, the wars over the "Holy Land" left between one-and-a-half million and two million people homeless.[71]

In 1979 there was a revolution in Iran. Under the leadership of Ayatollah Khomeini the revolution became an "Islamic Revolution" and the country

6145128/http://www.knesset.gov.il/elections/knesset15/elikud_m.htm.

66. Hosein, *Jerusalem in the Qur'an.*

67. "PLO Charter." Article 22, http://avalon.law.yale.edu/20th_century/plocov. asp#art22.

68. "The Avalon Project: Hamas Covenant 1988." Online: http://avalon.law.yale. edu/20th_century/hamas.asp.

69. Buzan, *Regions and powers,* 215.

70. "Total Casualties, Arab-Israeli Conflict." Online: https://www.jewishvirtualli-brary.org/jsource/History/casualtiestotal.html

71. "Arab-Israeli Conflict: Basic Facts." www.science.co.il/Arab-Israeli-conflict.asp⊠

became an "Islamic Republic." The Islamic Republican Party decided to establish an Islamic theocratic government and created a full-scale military force,[72] the Revolutionary Guard, to enforce it.[73]

Khomeini told Iranians, "do not use this term, 'democratic.' That is the Western style."[74] The National Democratic Front was banned in August 1979, the provisional government was disempowered in November, the Muslim People's Republican Party was barred in January 1980, a purge of universities was started in March 1980, and the leftist Islamist, Abolhassan Banisadr, was impeached in June 1981.[75]

Human rights groups estimated the number of casualties suffered by protesters and prisoners of the new system to be *several thousand.*

The first to be executed were members of the old system—senior generals, followed by over 200 senior civilian officials.[76] Brief trials lacking defense attorneys, juries, or opportunity for the accused to defend themselves,[77] were held by revolutionary judges such as Sadegh Khalkhali, the *Sharia* judge. By January 1980 "at least 582 persons had been executed." Among them was Amir Abbas Hoveida, former Prime Minister of Iran.[78]

Between January 1980 and June 1981, when Bani-Sadr was impeached, at least 900 executions took place,[79] for everything from drug and sexual offenses to "corruption on earth," from plotting counter-revolution and spying for Israel to membership in opposition groups.[80] In the year following that Amnesty International documented 2,946 executions, with several thousand more killed in the next two years according to the antigovernment guerillas, People's Mujahedin of Iran.[81]

The 1980–88 Iran-Iraq war began when Iraq invaded Iran. But most of the war was fought after Iran had regained the land it had lost and Iraq had offered a truce. Khomeini refused a ceasefire, proclaiming it was a

---

72. Mackey, *The Iranians*, 371.

73. Schirazi, *The Constitution of Iran*, 151.

74. Bakhash, *Reign of the Ayatollahs*, 73.

75. Ibid., 73.

76. Moin, *Khomeini: Life of the Ayatollah*, 208.

77. Bakhash, *Reign of the Ayatollahs*, 61.

78. Mackey, *The Iranians*, 291.

79. Bakhash, *Reign of the Ayatollahs*, 111.

80. Ibid., 111.

81. Ibid., 221–22.

"Holy War" and peace was only possible on two conditions: "the regime in Baghdad must fall and must be replaced by an Islamic Republic."[82]

Khomeini's "call to *jihad* incited thousands of young Iranian teenagers to volunteer for martyrdom missions."[83] His *Basij* volunteer militia movement "created" child and adult sacrifice as "holy soldiers,"[84] blessed by the Iranian mullahs' regime.[85]

The *Basiji* were best known for their suicidal "human wave attacks which cleared minefields or drew the enemy's fire."[86] It is estimated that tens of thousands of *Basiji* were killed in these suicidal human wave attacks and hundreds of thousands of other Iranians were killed in Khomeini's Holy War.[87]

*Basijis* were used in crackdowns in 1999, in 2003, and in the especially brutal 2009 crackdown on protesters in Iran.[88] Human rights activists have also charged that "the *Basij* militia men raped and murdered 26 year old Elnaz Babazadeh for 'wearing an improper dress.'"[89]

❧

The Muslim Brotherhood was founded in Egypt in 1928 as a religious social movement by the Islamic Scholar, Hassan al-Banna.[90] By the 1950s

---

82. Wright, *The Last Great Revolution*, 126.

83. Roshandil and Sharon, *Jihad and International Security*, 10.

84. Kuntzel, "Ahmadinejad's Demons, A Child of the Revolution Takes Over."

85. Singer, *Children at War*, 22; Brown, *Khomeini's Forgotten Sons*, 2; Armstrong, *The Battle for God*, 327–28.

86. "Basij Attacking People's Condo at Night." YouTube. June 17, 2009. Online: http://www.youtube.com/watch?v=RZae_Q-NpJE.

87. Singer, *Children at war*, 22.

88. Simone, "Feared Basij Militia has Deep History in Iranian Conflict." CNN. June 22, 2009. Online: http://edition.cnn.com/2009/WORLD/meast/06/22/iran.basij.militia.profile/index.html.

89. "IRAN: Judiciary Official Says Woman to be Stoned for Husband's Murder Not Just Adultery . . . ." *LA Times*, July 2010. Online: http://latimesblogs.latimes.com/babylonbeyond/2010/07/iran-stoning-sakineh-ashtiani.html.

90. Al-Mahdy, "The Muslim Brotherhood and the Egyptian State in the Balance of Democracy." Online: http://www.metransparent.com/old/texts/amin_el_mahdi_the_muslim_brotherhood_and_the_egyptian_state.htm. Kelly, "Egypt's Muslim Brotherhood Is Not to be Trusted." *Old Post-gazette*. January 22, 2012. Online: http://old.post-gazette.com/pg/12022/1204878-373-0.stm

41

the Muslim Brotherhood had an estimated two million members.[91] The Muslim Brotherhood started as a charitable organization, "preaching Islam, teaching the illiterate, setting up hospitals, and launching commercial enterprises." As its influence grew, the Muslim Brotherhood became more political, opposing British rule in Egypt.[92] Many Egyptian nationalists accuse the Muslim Brotherhood of violent killings during this period.[93]

Sayyed Qutb was a leader of the Muslim Brotherhood during the 1950s and 1960s and an Islamic theorist. Author of twenty-four books, he is best known for his book *Ma'alim fi al-Tariq* or Milestones, in which he argued that for Muslims to gain their freedom, a revolutionary vanguard would need to destroy *jahiliyyah*—the "state of ignorance" and its instruments—through a *jihad*, which he defined as a "resolute, offensive, violent struggle"[94] that would never end until it had eliminated everything non-Muslim from society.[95]

In 1966 Sayyed Qutb was convicted of the assassination of Egyptian President Nasser and was executed by hanging. But his legacy lived on. Sayyed influenced al-Qaeda through his writing and through his brother, Muhammad.[96] One of Muhammad Qutb's students was Ayman Zawahiri, who became a member of the Egyptian Islamic Jihad[97] and later a leading member of al-Qaeda and a mentor of Osama Bin Laden.[98]

Osama Bin Laden was a *wahabi*—a member of a strict puritanical sect practicing *takfir* (the condemnation of all Muslims they designated as "compromised," as "apostates") and *jihad*, which they also defined as a resolute, offensive, violent struggle against apostates.[99] Designating "compromised" Muslims as "apostates" not only gave Bin Laden's *jihadists* "a legal loophole around the prohibition of killing another Muslim," but actually

---

91. Hallett, *Africa Since 1875*, 138.

92. Delanoue, "Al-Ikhwānal-Muslimūn."

93. Chamieh, *Traditionalists, Militants and Liberal in Present Islam*, 140.

94. Qutb, *Milestones*, 63–69.

95. Ibid., 130, 134.

96. "Sayyid Qutb's Milestones (footnote 24)." Online: http://gemsofislamism.tripod.com/milestones_qutb.html#footnote_24

97. Atwan, *The Secret History of Al Qaeda*, 233.

98. Burke and Allen, "The five Ages of al-Qaida."

99. Sookhdeo, *Global Jihad*, 277.

turned that prohibition into "a religious obligation to execute" these apostate Muslims.[100]

The objectives of al-Qaeda include the ending American military presence in the Middle East and the Arabian Peninsula, overthrowing Arab regimes they consider corrupt and insufficiently religious,[101] and stopping American support for Israel.[102] Al-Qaeda has carried out six major terrorist attacks so far, four of them specifically against America.

> On December 29, 1992, al-Qaeda's first terrorist attack took place as two bombs were detonated in Aden, Yemen. The bombings were an attempt to eliminate American soldiers on their way to Somalia. No Americans were killed because the soldiers were staying in a different hotel. But the attack was the beginning of al-Qaeda's change from fighting armies to killing civilians. Two people were killed in the bombing, an Australian tourist and a Yemeni hotelier. Seven other Yemenis were severely injured.[103]

In 1993, "Ramzi Yousef used a truck bomb to attack the World Trade Center in New York City. Yousef, declared the attack was to "punish the U.S. for its support for the Israeli occupation of Palestinian territories."[104] The attack was meant to break the foundation of Tower One, knocking it into Tower Two, bringing the entire complex down. Yousef hoped this would kill at least 250,000 people. The towers shook but the foundation held; 1,042 people were injured, but he succeeded in killing only six people.[105]

In 1996, "Bin Laden personally engineered a plot to assassinate Clinton while the President was in Manila for the Asia-Pacific Economic Cooperation. However, intelligence agents intercepted a message just minutes before the motorcade was to leave, and alerted the US Secret Service, who discovered a bomb under a bridge."[106]

100. Eikmeier, "Qutbism: An Ideology of Islamic-Fascism," 89

101. Burke and Allen, "The five Ages of al-Qaida."

102. "1986–1992: CIA and British Recruit and Train Militants Worldwide to Help Fight Afghan War." Online: http://www.historycommons.org/context.jsp?item =a86operationcyclone.

103. Wright, *The Looming Tower*.

104. "February 1993 Bombing of the World Trade Center in New York City." Online: http://web.archive.org/web/20061207130217/http://cns.miis.edu/pubs/reports/wtc93. htm.

105. Ibid.

106. Leonard, "Osama Bin Laden Came within Minutes of Killing Bill Clinton."

In 1998 the US Embassy buildings in the East African cities of Dar es Salaam and Nairobi were bombed. The date of the bombings marked the eighth anniversary of the arrival of American forces in Saudi Arabia, which Osama Bin Laden vehemently and violently opposed. "In Dar es Salaam, at least 11 people were killed and 85 wounded; in Nairobi, at least 212 people were killed, and 4,000 wounded."[107]

In October 2000, al-Qaeda militants in Yemen bombed the missile destroyer U.S.S. Cole in a suicide attack, damaging the vessel and killing seventeen servicemen. Inspired by the success of the attack on the U.S.S Cole, al-Qaeda began to prepare for an attack on the U.S. itself.

On September 11, 2001, al-Qaeda coordinated multiple simultaneous attacks on the U.S.

> Evidence points to suicide squads led by al-Qaeda military commander Mohamed Atta as the commander of the attacks, with Bin Laden, Ayman al-Zawahiri, Khalid Sheikh Mohammed as the key planners and part of the political and military command.[108]

Two commercial airliners were flown into the World Trade Center towers, a third into The Pentagon, and a fourth, originally intended to target The Capitol, crashed in a field in Pennsylvania. These were the most devastating terrorist acts in American history, killing approximately 3,000 people.

The world watched as Bin Laden cried "Here is America struck by God Almighty in one of its vital organs, so its greatest buildings are destroyed."[109]

Bin Laden asserted that America was massacring Muslims in "Palestine, Chechnya, Kashmir and Iraq" and Muslims should retain the "right to attack in reprisal."[110]

On March 11, 2004, there were coordinated bombings against the commuter train system of Madrid, Spain. "The explosions killed 191 people and wounded another 1,800 people."[111] The attack in Madrid was explained as "inspired by al-Qaeda's call to punish Spain's government for supporting

---

107. "African Embassy Bombings." *Online News Hour*. PBS.org. Augsust 7, 1998. Online: http://www.pbs.org/newshour/bb/africa-july-dec98-bomb_8-7/

108 Lincoln, *Holy Terrors*, ?.

109. Lincoln, "The Rhetoric of Bush and Bin Laden", *Holy Terrors*. Online: https://mail.google.com/mail/u/0/?shva=1#inbox/14ab542543156511

110. Mir, "Osama Claims He Has Nukes."

111. "ElMundo." Online:http://www.elmundo.es/documentos/2006/04/11/auto_11m.html

the Iraq war," and "Al-Qaeda has called on *jihadists* to reconquer Spain as part of a Muslim caliphate, or kingdom under Islamic rule."[112]

❧

In response to the Soviet invasion of Afghanistan in 1979, Muslim rebels organized themselves into *jihadi* guerilla units, called *Mujahideen,* to fight against the Soviets.

Wilhelm Dietl, author of *Holy War*, recounts how "one *Mujahed* told him en route to an armed attack in Herat: '*We love to kill Russians and to be killed.*'"[113] My wife Ange was once invited by friends to an Afghan film night, in which *they proudly showed a home movie of Mujahideen crushing a live Soviet prisoner under a captured Soviet tank.*

After the Soviets withdrew in 1989, the *Mujahideen* fought each other for the control of the country in what became known as the Afghan Civil War.

One of the groups fighting against the invaders and then against *Mujahideen* were the *Taliban*—a group of "students" committed to the spreading of extreme revivalist Islam. The *Taliban* were a well-organized, fierce, fighting force, which gradually gained control and set up an Islamic Emirate, as the government of Afghanistan, from 1996 to 2001.

The Taliban committed systematic massacres against civilians. UN officials stated that there had been fifteen massacres between 1996 and 2001. The UN quotes "eyewitnesses in many villages describing Arab fighters carrying long knives used for slitting throats and skinning people."[114]

> On August 8, 1998 the Taliban launched an attack on Mazar-i-Sharif. Of 1500 defenders only 100 survived. Once in control, the Taliban began to kill people indiscriminately—shooting people in the street—target[ing] Hazaras. Women were raped, and thousands of people were locked in containers and left to suffocate. This "ethnic cleansing" left an estimated 5,000 to 6,000 dead.[115]

112. Sills, "Spanish Court to Deliver Verdict in Madrid Train Bombing Case."

113. Dietl, *Holy War*, 10.

114. "Taliban Massacres Outlined for UN." *Chicago Tribune,* October 12, 2001. Online: http://articles.chicagotribune.com/2001-10-12/news/0110120312_1_taliban-fighters-massacres-in-recent-years-mullah-mohammed-omar

115. Armajani, *Modern Islamist Movements*, 48.

45

"The Taliban's former ambassador to Pakistan, Mullah Abdul Salam Zaeef, stated that cruel behavior under and by the Taliban had been 'necessary.'"[116]

While they were in power the Taliban imposed an extreme interpretation of *Sharia* law, banning all music except the chanting of the Qur'an, beating men who trimmed their beards and barring women from all generic health, welfare, and educational services.

I remember a few years ago, while visiting colleagues working in Jalalabad under the Taliban, *a primary school teacher had his throat cut for teaching girls as well as boys in his class.* And just a few days ago, while writing this book, the Taliban *slaughtered 148 staff and students* across the border in Peshawar, Pakistan.

On the one hand, "the Taliban forced women into virtual house arrest, prohibiting them [from going outside their homes on their own] on pain of physical punishment."[117] Sohaila, a young woman who was convicted of walking with a man who was not a relative, was charged with adultery. She was publicly flogged in Ghazi Stadium and received 100 lashes.[118] On the other hand,

> several Taliban and Al-Qaeda commanders ran a network of human trafficking, abducting women and selling them into sex slavery. During one Taliban and Al-Qaeda offensive in 1999, more than 600 women were kidnapped. The targets for human trafficking were especially Tajik, Uzbek, and Hazara. Some women preferred to commit suicide over slavery, killing themselves.[119]

❖

In 2002 Mohammed Yousaf founded the Congregation of the People of Tradition for Proselytism and Jihad, better known as *Boko Haram* or "Western Education is Evil." It is "an Islamic *jihadist* and *takfiri* militant and terrorist organization based in the northeast of Nigeria, Cameroon, and Niger." The organization seeks to "put a stop to what it deems 'Westernization' and establish a 'pure' Islamic state ruled by Sharia law."[120]

116. Zaeef, "Taliban Spokesman: Cruel Behavior was Necessary."

117. "The Taliban's War on Women." Physicians for Human Rights, (August 1998). Online: https://www.law.georgetown.edu/rossrights/docs/reports/taliban.pdf.

118. Massoumi and AlSayyad, *The Fundamentalist City?* 223.

119. McGirk and Plain, "Lifting the Veil on Taliban Sex Slavery."

120. Walker, "What Is Boko Haram?"

The group is known for attacking Christians and government targets,[121] bombing churches, attacking schools and police stations,[122] kidnapping tourists, but has also assassinated members of the Islamic establishment.[123] Violence linked to the Boko Haram insurgency has resulted in 10,000 deaths between 2002 and 2013.[124]

During 2014, the world watched in horror as Boko Haram killed 122 residents in the city of Jos, more than 300 residents in Chikongudo near Gamboru Ngala, and kidnapped over 200 girls of Government Secondary School, Chibok, Borno State.[125]

In 2004 *Harakat al-Shabaab al-Mujahideen*—more commonly known as *al-Shabaab,* or "The Youth"—was founded as a jihadist group in Somalia. The group has also been suspected of having links with Boko Haram. In 2012, it joined the militant Islamicist organization al-Qaeda as a cell.[126] It seeks to impose strict forms of Sharia law.

> Al-Shabaab has also been accused of being responsible for the deaths of tens of thousands of elephants every year for their ivory, and for killing rangers hired to protect them. The proceeds from the ivory trade allegedly supply Al-Shabaab with income with which to carry out their operations.[127]

> On 21 September 2013, al-Shabab gunmen attacked the upmarket Westgate shopping mall in Nairobi Kenya. The assault lasted for three days and resulted in at least 67 deaths. Over 175 people were also wounded in the mass shooting.[128]

121. "Dozens Killed in Nigeria Clashes." *Al Jazeera,* December 24, 2011. Online: http://www.aljazeera.com/news/africa/2011/12/20111224124241652788.html.

122. "Nigeria: Dozens Dead in Church Bombings and Rioting." BBC, June 17, 2012. Online: http://www.aljazeera.com/news/africa/2011/12/20111224124241652788.html.

123. Campbell, "Should U.S. Fear Boko Haram?"

124. Campbell, *Nigeria: Dancing on the Brink,* 139.

125. "Nigeria Violence: 'Boko Haram' Destroy Village." BBC, May 22, 2014. Online: http://www.bbc.com/news/world-africa-27526620.

126. "Al-Shabaab Joining al Qaeda, Monitor Group Says." CNN, February 9, 2012. Online: http://edition.cnn.com/2012/02/09/world/africa/somalia-shabaab-qaeda/

127. Stewart, "Illegal Ivory Trade Funds al-Shabaab's Terrorist Attacks."

128. York, "Analysis of al-Shabaab's Attack at the Westgate Mall in Nairobi, Kenya." (November 2013). Online: http://s3.documentcloud.org/documents/894158/westgate-report-for-shield-website.pdf.

The previous conflict in Darfur, Sudan, is interpreted as "Holy War" by the government in Khartoum.[129]

> Two rebel movements—the Sudan Liberation Army (SLA) and the Justice and Equality Movement (JEM)—took up arms against the Sudanese government, complaining about the marginalization of the area and the failure to protect farmers from attacks by nomads. The government of Sudan responded by unleashing Arab militias known as *Janjaweed*, or "devils on horseback." *Sudanese military forces and Janjaweed militia attacked hundreds of villages throughout Darfur. Over 400 villages were completely destroyed and millions of civilians were forced to flee their homes.*[130]

> In the ongoing genocide, African farmers in Darfur are being systematically displaced and murdered at the hands of the Janjaweed. The genocide in Darfur has claimed 400,000 lives and displaced over 2,500,000 people. More than one hundred people continue to die each day; five thousand die every month.[131]

In June 2005, the International Criminal Court (ICC) launched investigations into human rights violations in Darfur. Accused of genocide, Sudanese President Omar al Bashir threatened "to mount a *jihad* against United Nations peacekeepers."[132] On March 4, 2009, President Omar al Bashir, became *the first sitting president to be indicted by ICC for directing a campaign of mass killing, rape, and pillage against civilians.*[133]

In the Philippines the most active extreme Islamist terrorist groups are the Abu Sayyaf, the Rajah Sulaim Movement, the Moro Islamic Liberation Front, and *Jemaah Islamiyah.* Since January 2000 Islamist terrorist groups in the Philippines have carried out over forty major bombings against civilians and civilian property, mostly in the southern regions of the country

129. Frey, *Genocide and International Justice Global Issues,* 365.

130. "Genocide in Dafur." United Human Rights Council. Online: http://www.unitedhumanrights.org/genocide/genocide-in-sudan.htm

131. Ibid.

132. Gettleman, "Sudanese Leader Mounts Charm Offensive."

133. "Genocide in Dafur." United Human Rights Council. Online: http://www.unitedhumanrights.org/genocide/genocide-in-sudan.htm

around Mindano, Basilan, and Jolo,[134] and numerous bombings have also been carried out in and around Metro Manila. In the period from 2000 to 2007 attacks "killed nearly 400 and wounded well over 1,500 Filipino civilians."[135]

In Indonesia the most active terrorist groups were *Laskar Jihad* and *Jemaah Islamiyah*. *Laskar Jihad* has called Indonesian Muslims "to wage a holy war" into Indonesia's Moluccan islands, and carried out anti-Christian attacks in Sulawesi.[136] *Laskar Jihad* was also involved in the 1999 violence against Christians in East Timor.[137] "It has been called Indonesia's Dirty Little Holy War Holy Terror."[138]

Terrorism in Indonesia intensified in 2000 with the Jakarta Stock Exchange bombing, followed by four more large attacks. On October 12, 2002 *Jemaah Islamiyah* organized the bombings in the tourist district of Kuta on the Indonesian island of Bali. "The attack killed 202 people (including 88 Australians, 38 Indonesians, 27 Britons, 7 Americans, 6 Swedes, 3 Danes). A further 240 were injured."[139]

An audio-cassette purportedly carrying a recorded voice message from Osama Bin Laden stated that the Bali bombings were in direct retaliation for support of the United States' war on terror and Australia's role in the liberation of East Timor.[140]

In 2014, ISIL, The Islamic State of Iraq and the Levant, otherwise known as ISIS, the Islamic State of Iraq and Syria (or the Islamic State of Iraq and al-Sham), now called simply IS, the Islamic State, emerged as a significant militant political movement.[141] IS is a "self-proclaimed Caliphate, it claims

134. "Lives Destroyed: Attacks on Civilians in the Philippines." Human Rights Watch, July 2007. Online: http://www.hrw.org/reports/2007/philippines0707/index.htm.

135. Conde, "400 Killed by Terrorism in Philippines since 2000."

136. Elegant, "Indonesia's Dirty Little Holy War."

137. "Who are the Laskar Jihad?" BBC News Asia-Pacific, June 20, 2000. Online: http://content.time.com/time/world/article/0,8599,187655,00.html

138. Elegant, "Indonesia's Dirty Little Holy War."

139. "Suicide Bomber Praying as He Detonates Bomb: Survivor" *The Jakarta Globe*, April 15, 2011. Online: http://thejakartaglobe.beritasatu.com/archive/suicide-bomber-praying-as-he-detonates-bomb-survivor/435595/

140. Arnaz, "Update: Explosion Was Suicide Attack."

141. Withnall, "Iraq Crisis."

religious authority over all Muslims and aspires to bring much of the Muslim-inhabited regions of the world under its direct political control," beginning with Iraq and Syria and taking in "territory in the Levant, which includes Jordan, Israel, Palestine, Lebanon, Kuwait, Cyprus and southern Turkey."[142]

The group, in its original form, was supported by a variety of Sunni insurgent groups, including its predecessor organizations, the Mujahideen Shura, the Islamic State of Iraq (ISI), Al-Qaeda in Iraq (AQI), the insurgent groups Jaysh al-Fatiheen, Jund al-Sahaba, Katbiyan Ansar Al-Tawhid wal Sunnah, and a number of Sunni Iraqi tribes. ISIS grew as an organization owing to its participation in the Syrian Civil War and the strength of its supreme leader, Abu Bakr al-Baghdadi. Economic and political discrimination against Iraqi Sunnis since the fall of Saddam Hussein also helped it to gain support.[143]

ISIS is known for "its harsh Wahabist interpretation of Islam"[144] and "brutal violence"[145] directed at Shia Muslims and Christians in particular.[146] It has 4,000 fighters (including Australians[147]) who, in addition to attacks on military targets, "have claimed responsibility for attacks that have killed thousands of civilians."[148] ISIS had close links with al-Qaeda until 2014, but in February al-Qaeda cut all ties with the group, reportedly for its "notorious intractability" and wanton brutality.[149]

During the Iraqi conflict in 2014, ISIS released videos showing its ill treatment of civilians, many of whom had apparently been targeted on the basis of their religion or ethnicity. "From 5 to 22 June, ISIS killed more than 1,000 Iraqi civilians and injured more than 1,000."[150] ISIS has released

142. "Islamic State of Iraq and al-Sham" *The Wall Street Journal*, June 12, 2014. Online: http://blogs.wsj.com/briefly/2014/06/12/islamic-state-of-iraq-and-al-sham-the-short-answer/

143. "Islamic State of Iraq and al-Sham."

144. Bulos, "Islamic State of Iraq and Syria aims to recruit Westerners with video."

145. McCoy, "ISIS, Beheadings and the Success of Horrifying Violence."

146. Abi-Habib, "Iraq's Christian Minority Feels Militant Threat."

147. Bender, "Australia Is the Largest Per Capita Contributor of Foreign Fighters to ISIS."

148. Al-Salhy, "Al Qaeda tightens Grip on Western Iraq in Bid for Islamic State."

149. Sly, "Al-Qaeda Disavows Any Ties with Radical Islamist ISIS Group in Syria, Iraq."

150. "ISIL Militants Killed More Than 1000 Civilians." *RTT News*, June 24, 2014. Online: http://www.rttnews.com/2340932/isil-militants-killed-more-than-1000-civilians-in-recent-onslaught-in-iraq-un.aspx

photographs of its fighters "shooting scores of young men in cold-blooded 'executions' [that] amounted to war crimes."[151] According to one report, ISIS's capture of Iraqi cities in June 2014 included an upsurge in crimes against women, including kidnap and rape.[152]

> Christians who want to remain in the "caliphate" that the Islamic State declared (July 2014) in parts of Iraq and Syria must agree to abide by terms of a *dhimma* contract. "We offer them three choices: Islam; the *dhimma* contract—involving payment of jizya; if they refuse this they will have nothing but the sword."[153]

Senior British Imams have come together to decree ISIS as an illegitimate group who do not represent Islam in any way. "We are Muslims united against ISIS, against terrorism, against atrocity, against suffering," says Sayed Ali Rizvi, head of the Majlis Ulama-e-Shia group. "As a Sunni Muslim, I do not accept the Caliphate of ISIS—ISIS is a terrorist organization," said Maulana Shahid Raza, of Leicester Central Mosque. Abu Muntasir, chief executive of the Muslim charity organization, JIMAS, said, "Brothers and sisters, if I could tell you one [thing] about ISIS I would tell you that they are evil, they are corrupt, they are self-seeking, self-centered, vicious people. Don't get mixed up with them."[154]

Recently Australian Imams have denounced ISIS. Dr Mohamed Abdalla, acting Imam of the Kuraby Mosque, said, "the leaders of the community are united against violence." We "are making an unequivocal, clear statement that we're against violence, we're against acts of terror, regardless of who perpetrates these acts."[155]

But, even as they were denouncing ISIS, a self-styled sheik gunman, Man Haron Monis, took seventeen people hostage in a televised seventeen hour siege at the Lindt Cholocat Café in Martin Place, that ended in a hail of bullets, leaving four wounded and two dead, in the name of ISIS, at the heart of downtown Sydney.

And so it goes on and on.

---

151. Spencer, "Iraq Crisis: UN Condemns 'War Crimes' as Another Town Falls to Isis."

152. Radwan and Blumenfeld, "Surging Violence against Women in Iraq."

153. Evans and al-Rube'l, "Convert, Pay Tax, or Die Islamic State Warns Christians."

154. Hafiz, "Sunni and Shiite British Imams Denounce ISIS Together in New Video."

155. Withey and Mellor, "Brisbane Mosque Service Brings Christian and Muslim Leaders Together."

# 3

## Reflecting On Our "Not-So-Holy" So-Called "Holy Wars"

Christians and Muslims make up over half the world's population. So it is absolutely vital for the future welfare of the human family that we examine our frequent utter disregard for human rights, diabolical persecution of unorthodox traditions and heterodox religions, and total destruction of "infidels" in genocidal "Holy Wars" waged in the name of our "great God."

In the light of our overview of our not-so-holy Christian and Muslim "Holy Wars" the atrocities are undeniable. And, in my experience, Christians and Muslims don't tend to deny them. However, they do tend to discount them: either by generally emphasizing the positive influence, rather than the negative effect of their religion; or by explaining that, in each case of an atrocity committed by a believer, there were a particular set of extenuating circumstances that make the act "understandable," if not "excusable."

For example, if you say something about the Crusades or the Inquisition, most Christians will say things like: "it was a long time ago," "times were different then," "people didn't know any better," "the people who committed those crimes against humanity must have been crazy," "they weren't really Christians, you know," "if you want to know what real Christianity is all about, forget the Crusades and the Inquisition and consider the example of Mother Teresa and the Missionaries of Charity." Or if you say something about the *Mujahideen* or the *Taliban*, most Muslims will say things like: "it is an other country," "the culture is different there," "people don't know any better," "the people who commit those crimes against humanity must be crazy," "they aren't really Muslims, you know," "if you want to know what real Islam is all about, forget the *Mujahideen* and the *Taliban*, and consider the example of Abdul Ghaffar Khan and the *Khudai Khidmatgar*."

None of these comments actually deny the fact that atrocities were committed in the name of Christianity or Islam. But they do attempt to discount the significance of these atrocities as true indicators of the nature of Christianity or Islam.

Now this brings us face to face with the life and death question, at the very heart of the matter, that we desperately need to answer. Are the atrocities that are done in the name of Christianity or Islam true indicators of the nature of Christianity or Islam, or not?

If the answer to this question is that these atrocities are not true indicators—but mere aberrations—then we have nothing to fear from the continued expansion of Christianity or Islam. But, if the answer to this question is, as I suspect, that these cruelties are true indicators—and inevitable consequences—of the way we have constructed our religions, then we have everything to fear from Christianity or Islam in the coming millennium.

To answer this question we will need to consider a range of personal, political, and spiritual perspectives, then, assess how significant Christianity or Islam, as religions, are as the "real" explanations of the cause of these not-so-holy Christian and Muslim "Holy Wars."

## Personal Factors—Evil, Fear, Avarice, Power, and Authoritarian Personalities

All the "personal interpretations" of atrocities done in the name of religion suggest the "real" explanation has more to do with people's personalities than their religion.

Philip Zimbardo says evil is "knowing better and doing worse." He says "evil consists in intentionally behaving in ways that harm, abuse, demean, dehumanize, or destroy innocent others—or using one's authority to encourage or permit others to do so on your behalf."[1]

The psychiatrist, Scott Peck, suggests that there are some people who are actually evil. People who are evil, Peck says, are those "who refuse to face their own sin, project blame on to others, and scapegoat others to such an extent that they will use whatever power they have at their disposal to destroy the objects of their blame."[2]

1. Zimbardo, *The Lucifer Effect*, 5
2. Peck, *The People of the Lie*, 69

Timur from the fourteenth century and Hitler from the twentieth century immediately come to mind. When Timur captured "idolatrous" Hindus, he put them to the sword with no mercy. "Before the battle for Delhi, Timur executed more than one hundred thousand Hindu captives." and "cities were rid of their Hindu male population through systematic mass slaughters."[3]

When Hitler had his chance to deal with the "filthy Jews," Jewish men, women, and children were tagged with yellow stars, then dragged out, beaten up, and shot, or rounded up like animals, thrown onto cattle trucks, and herded into concentration camps, where six million of them were exterminated in "the worst single atrocity that our world has ever known."

❖

Both Timur and Hitler are classic cases of archetypal pathological scapegoating evil. But neither of them could have executed their plans without "willing executioners," people who accepted their authority, assisted with their activities, shared their resources with their agencies, and subordinated themselves to their directives, aiding and abetting them.

And not all those involved in aiding and abetting them in these atrocities we are reflecting on could be considered "evil" in the classical pathological sense that we are speaking about.

What makes ordinary people, like you and me, who aid and abet in such atrocities, do the evil that they do? Well, according to Hannah Arendt, the answer to the question is actually quite banal. It is our willingness to support the evil that these men do out of a sense of obligation, a habit of obedience, the desire for approval, the hope of reward, the fear of punishment, or perhaps just plain laziness—taking the path of least resistance.[4]

❖

Some people may get caught up in the perpetration of these offences out of fear.

Humans have a "basic need to belong, to associate with and be accepted by others central to family bonding and community building." And "the basic desire to be 'in' and not 'out' is a powerful force, that can

3. Elliot, *The History of India*, 389.
4. Sharp, *Power and Struggle*, 11–12, 18–24.

transform human behavior, pushing people across the boundary between good and evil just to feel like they are 'in' rather than 'out.'"[5] "The 'terror of being left outside,' the fear of rejection when one wants acceptance, can negate personal autonomy. The imagined threat of being cast out into that out-group can lead some people to do virtually anything to avoid their terrifying rejection.... It makes people willing to suffer painful initiation rites" and/or commit horrendous crimes.[6] C. S. Lewis, speaking of the desire for people to be part of an exclusive inner circle, said in "The Inner Ring": "Of all the passions, the passion for the Inner Ring is the most [powerful factor] in making a man who is not yet very bad do very bad things."[7]

You could argue that Augustine had Pelagius excommunicated because he was not only afraid of Pelagius, but also afraid of the implications of Pelagian doctrine. So Augustine had Pelagius cast out of the Inner Ring.

Sayyed Qutb had a great passion for the Inner Ring of Islam. In his book *Ma'alim fi al-Tariq* or Milestones he argued that for Muslims to gain their freedom, a revolutionary vanguard would need to destroy *jahiliyyah*—the "state of ignorance" and its instruments—which would never end until it had eliminated everything non-Muslim from society.[8] And the fear of being labeled as "disloyal" to this Inner Ring of Islam, has been used by terrorist groups to secure the "loyalty" of their recruits to their commanders and their total commitment to obey all their commands.[9]

Some people may get caught up in the perpetration of these offences through avarice.

The Umayyads set up the *dhimmah* to increase taxes from the *dhimmis* (non-Muslim subjects) to explicitly benefit the Arab Muslim community financially. Many Muslim rulers preferred non-Muslim subjects to stay non-Muslims and tax them rather than convert them. "Governors lodged

---

5. Lewis, "The Inner Ring Memorial Lecture."

6. Ibid.

7. Ibid.

8. Qutb, *Milestones*, 130, 134.

9. Ibid., 63–69. Religious Rehabilitation Group, "Our Message." Online: http://www.rrg.sg/index.php?option=com_content&view=article&id=15%3Aour-message&catid=2%3Aour-message&Itemid=6&limitstart=6

complaints with the caliph when he enacted laws that made conversion easier, depriving the provinces of revenues (from the *dhimmis*).[10]

Inquisitors grew very rich very quickly. "They received bribes from the wealthy who escaped accusation." And they "confiscated the property of the accused." Inquisitors rarely shared their ill-gotten gains with the episcopal courts. They "seize[d] everything for [them]selves, not even sending a share to the officials of the Inquisition at Rome."[11]

෴

Some people may get caught up in the perpetration of these offences in order to acquire power.

Conquerors like Salman b. Rabi'a al-Bahili under orders of al-Walid b. 'Uqba, "went into the land of Armenia killing and taking prisoners and plunder. Then, his hands laden [with plunder] he left and returned to al-Walid."[12]

"Sultan Mehmed issued an order [that the city be] plundered. From all directions they [the *gazis*] came. . . . They entered the city, passed the infidels over the sword [i.e. slaughtered them], . . . slew the miserable common people. . . . [and] placed [survivors] in chains, placed metal rings round their necks."[13]

Conquistadors like Francisco Pizarro captured the Emperor Atahuapa and kept him as a hostage to control the Inca Empire. In spite of paying a vast ransom, including "one room full of gold and two rooms full of silver," Atahuapa was killed, and all Inca opposition, like all Aztec opposition, was crushed.[14] Hernando Cortes could arrogantly brag about becoming "the most powerful man in the New World," owning "more than twenty thousand slaves" whose sole purpose in life was simply to do his bidding.[15]

෴

Some people may get caught up because of authoritarian personalities.

10. Astren, *Karaite Judaism and Historical Understanding*, 33.

11. Ellerbe, *The Dark Side of Christian History*, 4.

12. Yar-Shater, "The Crisis of the Early Caliphate," 9.

13. Ibid., 80.

14. Andrews, *Christi-Anarchy*, 34.

15. Ibid., 34.

It could be said that "if there is a cause for war in our genes, then the 'authoritarian personality' is its manifestation. This personality type is expressed by rigidity of views, to see all things in black and white, a strong desire to be told what to do, an equally strong desire to tell 'lesser mortals' what to do."[16]

A German philosopher, Theodor Adorno, was the first to define the "authoritarian personality." He said that: "While finding comfort in the identification of submissive behavior towards authority, the authoritarian person directs his/her aggression towards other groups, often racial (and/or religious) minorities."[17]

The British psychiatrist, Jack Dominion, suggests that an "authoritarian personality" tends to be "more secure when he has his niche within a hierarchy, is submissive and respectful to those above him, and contemptuous and dictatorial to those below him, repressive of his own instincts, is generally in favor of discipline, and is punitive towards 'sinners,' particularly if they are judged to be 'inferior' in any way."[18]

A classic example of a Christian authoritarian personality was Oliver Cromwell. The notorious English Puritan leader, Oliver Cromwell, razed the ancient city of Drogheda to the ground, slaughtered its "papist" Irish inhabitants, and rejoiced in the "righteous judgment of God" he had been able to bring "upon these barbarous wretches."[19]

A classic example of a Muslim authoritarian personality was Ayatollah Khomeini. The infamous Iranian "Islamist" dictator, Ayatollah Khomeini declared the "Holy War" on Iraq and peace only possible on the condition: "the regime in Baghdad must fall and must be replaced by an Islamic Republic."[20] His "call to [violent] jihad, created child and adult sacrifice as 'holy soldiers.'"[21] Tens of thousands of these were killed in suicidal human wave attacks and hundreds of thousands of other Iranians were killed in Khomeini's "Holy War."[22]

---

16. "Authoritarian Personality—Extremism." In *A Road to Peace*. Online: http://www.roadtopeace.org/research.php?itemid=366

17. Ibid.

18. Dominion, *Authority*, 11.

19. Kreider and Yoder, "Christians and War," 24.

20. Wright, *The Last Great Revolution*, 126.

21. Küntzel, "Ahmadinejad's Demons."

22. Rawshandil and Chadha, *Jihad and International Security*, 10.

According to Dominion, "it does not require much imagination to see that such authoritarian personalities" as Oliver Cromwell and Ayatollah Khomeini, would use religious language, symbols, and rituals "to support just about everything that would have been repudiated as a proper . . . attitude by the originator of that faith."[23]

## Political Factors—Evil, Hysteria, Charisma, Sanctions, and Authoritarian Societies

All the political interpretations of atrocities done in the name of religion would suggest the real explanation has more to do with people's politics than their religion.

I would suggest that people can be evil, not only personally, but also politically. In fact, I would argue that such "evil—is the exercise of political power that imposes one's will upon others, by overt or covert coercion, without due regard for love and justice."[24]

One example of the epitome of personal and political evil was when a cluster of small Italian towns sought to throw off the yoke of the tyranny of the Catholic Church in 1375, the pope's legate in Italy, Robert of Geneva, hired an army of mercenaries, and set about taking revenge on the little town of Cessna.

> Swearing clemency by a solemn oath on his cardinal's hat, Cardinal Robert persuaded the men of Cessna to lay down their arms, and won their confidence by asking for fifty hostages and immediately releasing them as evidence of good will. Then summoning his mercenaries . . . he ordered a general massacre "to exercise justice." For three days and nights, beginning February 3, 1377, while the city gates were closed, the soldiers slaughtered. "All the squares were full of dead." Trying to escape, hundreds drowned in the moats, thrust back by relentless swords. Women were seized for rape, ransom was placed on children, plunder succeeded the killing, "and what could not be carried away, they burned, made

23. Ibid., 12.
24. Andrews, *Building a Better World*, 115.

unfit for use, or spilled upon the ground." The toll of the dead was between 2,500 and 5,000.[25]

Another example of the epitome of personal and political evil is the "Holy War" conducted by the government of Omar al Bashir.[26] He unleashed Arab militias known as *Janjaweed*, or "devils on horseback." The *Janjaweed* militia attacked hundreds of villages throughout Darfur. In the ongoing genocide, African farmers in Darfur are being systematically displaced and murdered at the hands of the Janjaweed. The genocide in Darfur has claimed 400,000 lives and displaced over 2,500,000 people. Consequently, President Omar al Bashir has been indicted by ICC for directing the campaign of mass killing, rape, and pillage against civilians in Darfur.[27]

❧

These atrocities could not have taken place without "willing executioners," people who accept authority, assist with activities, share their resources with agencies, and subordinate themselves to these evil political directives, aiding and abetting them.

What makes people who aid and abet in these atrocities do the evil that they do? Inner determinants, like an "evil" disposition, or outer determinants, like an "evil" situation?

Traditionally people have argued that it is inner determinants like disposition that makes the difference. Some people are good. But some people are bad. Bad people sow bad seeds that sooner or later inevitably produce bad fruit. In this view evil is "essential." It is an inherent quality that characterizes evil people. Alternatively people have argued that outer determinants make the difference. We all have the capacity for good and evil. The situation we are in is more likely to affect the outcome than our disposition.[28]

❧

Some people may get caught up in the perpetration of these offences through hysteria.

25. Tuchman, *A Distant Mirror*, 322.

26. Frey, *Genocide and International Justice*, 365.

27. Ibid.

28. Zimbardo, *The Lucifer Effect*, 7.

Elias Canetti, in his book *Crowds and Power*, analyses the way in which ordinary people can be caught up in a crowd, and, through crowd hysteria which simultaneously increases their sense of power, and decreases their sense of responsibility. Under such situations people can commit extraordinary crimes against humanity—which I witnessed in the 1984 Delhi massacres.[29]

In the Middle Ages in England, where there was no official program for prosecuting witches, many women were still killed by mobs. A common practice was to "swim a witch" in which a mob would take a woman, accused of witchcraft, bind her hand and feet, and throw her into some water to see if she could "swim." If the woman was rejected by the water, the medium of holy baptism, and floated to the top, she would be pronounced guilty, and would be killed by the mob. If the woman was embraced by the holy waters, and sank to the bottom, she would be pronounced innocent, and would be posthumously acclaimed by the mob. Either way the hysterical crowd got their corpse.[30]

In *The Stoning of Soraya M.*, "a shocking true drama, expos[ing] the dark power of mob rule" in Iran, Zahra tells "a harrowing tale . . . about [the stoning of] her niece, Soraya: . . . a story which involves a town all too easily led down a path of deceit, coercion, and hysteria."[31] In another video of the actual Stoning of Siddqa, in Afghanistan, featured on the BBC, the nineteen-year-old, charged with "run[ning] away [with her lover] after being sold into an arranged marriage for $9,000 against her will," is pitilessly pulverized under a bombardment of rocks, to the frenzied cheers of a hysterical crowd, feverishly crying out *"Allahu Akbar."*[32]

Some people may get caught up in the perpetration of these offences because they were dazzled by the charisma of a dynamic leader who insisted that they got involved.

29. Canetti, *Crowds and Power*.

30. Thomas, *Religion and the Decline of Magic*, 551.

31 "The Stoning of Soraya M." Online: http://www.mpowerpictures.com/films/the_stoning_of_soraya_m/

32. "Stoned to Death with Her Lover." *Daily Mail Australia*, January 28, 2011. Online: http://www.dailymail.co.uk/news/article-1350945/Horrific-video-emerges-Taliban-fighters-stoning-couple-death-adultery.html#ixzz2zymVvBao

Max Weber, in his *Theory of Social and Economic Organizations*, says that leaders with charisma have an aura of magic about them, and that people can be so strongly attracted to this charisma, this powerful personal magnetism, that, to their devotees, such leaders may prove to be irresistible.[33]

Efrain Rios Montt was a charismatic leader. Just ask his pastor. "He is a king; a new King David, who will defeat the enemy and lead the chosen ones to victory!" So if he says it's necessary to "massacre the Indians" (in order to "massacre the demons," because "the Indians are demon possessed") then it must be necessary to massacre the Indians.[34]

Osama Bin Laden was an extremely charismatic leader. He presented as a genuine, pious, courageous *jihadi* who used his wealth in the service of Islam and apparently charmed the people who met him with his magnetism. He was able to attract support from people, even with a $25 million bounty on his head promised to anyone who would betray him. And he was able to arouse a full measure of devotion and dedication from his supporters, to the point of their being willing to die in the process of killing his enemies.[35]

❦

Some people may get caught up in the perpetration of these offences because they were driven by the sanctions they were threatened with if they did not get involved.

Gene Sharp, in his book, *Power and Struggle*, analyses the way that subjects can be compelled by the rulers, who have power over them, to act in compliance with a directive, even when it contravenes every standard of common human decency. After all, "sanctions," he says, "are an enforcement of obedience."[36]

Excommunication is a sanction used to great effect by religious communities through the centuries. However, execution has always been the ultimate sanction used as a last resort to enforce total unquestioning obedience to religious authorities.

---

33. Weber, *The Theory of Social and Economic Organizations*.

34. Diamond, *Spiritual Warfare*, 166.

35. Silinsky, "Jihad's Charism."

36. Sharp, *Power and Struggle*, 12.

The Inquisitor, Francisco Pena, proclaimed, "We must remember that the main purpose of trail and execution is not to save the soul of the accused but to . . . put fear into others!"[37] The Moghul, Aurangzeb, "[laid] waste the country [in the North and Central India], destroying temples, making prisoners of the women and children of the infidels, . . ."[38] commanding Hindus in the North-West Frontier to convert or be executed. An Afghan friend once told me how he was captured by the Taliban, and then ordered by the commander, on pain of death, to take part in a pitiless, unprovoked attack on his own village.[39]

❧

Some people may get caught up in the perpetration of these offences because they were directed to by authoritarian societies that dictated the way they lived their lives.

Juan Linz described authoritarian societies as political systems characterized by a legitimacy based on conviction and emotion, especially the identification of the regime as "a necessary evil" to combat "enemies"; limited constraints or checks and balances on the regime; prohibition of anti-regime activity; and repression of regime opponents.[40]

Traditional authoritarian societies are those "in which the ruling authority," generally a single person, is maintained in power "through a combination of appeals to traditional legitimacy, patron-client ties, and repression, which is carried out by an apparatus bound to the ruling authority through personal loyalties, while modern authoritarian societies also include a coalition of the military and/or the bureaucracy who collaborate with the ruling authority to systematically impose the regime and repress opponents."[41]

Where authoritarian societies frame their authority in religious terms these systems of control have immense power over our lives.[42] They claim they have "a God-given right" to control because, they say, that as "properly constituted authorities" they are the "God-anointed, God-appointed

37. Kamen, *Inquisition and Society in Spain*, 161.

38. Khan, "Muntakhabu-l Lubab," 300.

39. Sookhdeo, *Global Jihad*, 243.

40. Casper, *Fragile Democracies*, 40–50.

41. Gasiorowski, "The Political Regimes Project," 110–11.

42. McAlpine, *Facing the Powers*, 15.

guardians of our lives."[43] And we are taught to submit to their "God-given" authority, so "we can learn from God through them," as it says in a lesson I saw distributed in a religious instruction class at a local school in my area.[44]

In 1961, three months after the start of the trial of the Holocaust administrator, Adolf Eichmann, Stanley Milgram devised his (in)famous psychological study to answer the question: "Was it that Eichmann and his accomplices had mutual intent, with regard to the goals of the Holocaust?" Or was it that Eichmann was simply trained to take orders?

Milgram measured the willingness of participants to obey an authority figure, who instructed them to perform acts that conflicted with their personal conscience. Milgram's tests showed it could have been that the millions of accomplices were merely following orders, despite violating their deepest moral beliefs. The experiments have been repeated many times, with different percentages across the globe, but with remarkably consistent results within societies.[45]

> The volunteer subject was given the role of teacher, and the confederate (an actor), the role of learner. The participants drew slips of paper to "determine" their roles. Unknown to the subject, both slips said "teacher," and the actor claimed to have the slip that read "learner," thus guaranteeing that the participant would always be the "teacher." At this point, the "teacher" and "learner" were separated into different rooms where they could communicate but not see each other. In one version of the experiment, the confederate was sure to mention to the participant that he had a heart condition.

The "teacher" was given an electric shock from the electro-shock generator as a sample of the shock that the "learner" would supposedly receive during the experiment. The "teacher" was then given a list of word pairs, which he was to teach the learner. The teacher began by reading the list of word pairs to the learner. The teacher would then read the first word of each pair and read four possible answers. The learner would press a button to indicate his response. If the answer was incorrect, the teacher would administer a shock to the learner, with the voltage increasing in 15-volt

43. Ibid., 12.

44. Lesson Outline, Brisbane State High School. Undated.

45. Milgram first described his research in 1963 in an article published in the *Journal of Abnormal and Social Psychology*, and later discussed his findings in greater depth in his 1974 book, *Obedience to Authority: An Experimental View.*

increments for each wrong answer. If correct, the teacher would read the next word pair.

The subjects believed that for each wrong answer, the learner was receiving actual shocks. In reality, there were no shocks. After the confederate was separated from the subject, the confederate set up a tape recorder integrated with the electro-shock generator, which played pre-recorded sounds for each shock level. After a number of voltage level increases, the actor started to bang on the wall that separated him from the subject. After several times banging on the wall and complaining about his heart condition, all responses by the learner would cease.

At this point, many people indicated a desire to stop the experiment and check on the learner. Some test subjects paused at 135 volts and began to question the purpose of the experiment. However, after being assured that they would not be held responsible, most continued. A few subjects began to laugh nervously or exhibit other signs of extreme stress once they heard the screams of pain coming from the learner.

If at any time the subject indicated his desire to halt the experiment, he was given a succession of verbal prods by the experimenter (authority figure), in this order:

- Please *continue*

- The experiment requires that you *continue*

- It is absolutely essential that you *continue*

- You have no other choice, you *must* go on

If the subject still wished to stop after all four successive verbal prods, the experiment was halted. Otherwise, it was halted after the subject had given the "lethal" maximum 450-volt shock three times in succession.

Before conducting the experiment, Milgram polled fourteen Yale University senior-year psychology majors to predict the behavior of 100 hypothetical teachers. All of the poll respondents believed that only a very small fraction of teachers (the range was from zero to three out of one hundred, with an average of 1.2) would be prepared to inflict the maximum voltage. Milgram also informally polled his colleagues and found that they too believed very few subjects would progress beyond a very strong shock.

In Milgram's first set of experiments, 65 percent (twenty-six out of forty) of experiment participants administered the experiment's final massive 450-volt shock, though many were very uncomfortable doing so; at some point, every participant paused and questioned the experiment, some said they would refund the money they were paid for participating in the experiment.

Milgram summarized the experiment in his 1974 article, "The Perils of Obedience," writing:

> I set up a simple experiment at Yale to test how much pain an ordinary citizen would inflict on another person simply because he was ordered to by an experimental scientist. Stark authority was pitted against the subjects' strongest moral imperatives against hurting others, and, with the subjects' ears ringing with the screams of the victims, authority won more often than not.
>
> The chief finding of the study [is] the extreme willingness of adults to go to almost any lengths on the command of an authority. Ordinary people, simply doing their jobs, and without any particular hostility on their part, can become agents in a terrible destructive process. Moreover, even when the destructive effects of their work become patently clear, and they are asked to carry out actions incompatible with fundamental standards of morality, relatively few people have the resources needed to resist authority.[46]

Dr. Thomas Blass of the University of Maryland, Baltimore County, performed a meta-analysis on the results of repeated performances of the experiment. He found that the percentage of participants who are prepared to inflict fatal voltages remains remarkably constant, 61–66 percent, regardless of time or place. And none of the participants who refused to administer the final shocks left the room to check the health of the victim without requesting permission to leave—and not one insisted that the experiment itself be terminated when they left.

The ten ways in which Stanley Milgram got good people to do evil was simply to:

1. Negotiate a contractual obligation

2. Assign valued roles with set scripts

3. Make rules that require obedience

4. Frame "hurting people" as "helping"

5. Take responsibility for their actions

6. Work towards ultimate evil bit by bit

7. Then move them on "a little bit more"

46. Milgram, "The Perils of Obedience."

8. Subtly move from being just to unjust

9. Make the price of resistance too much

10. Use "the big lie" to justify evil as good.[47]

In 1974 J. Carlson used his class at the University of Hawaii to test the willingness of 570 psychology students to endorse the "final solution"—the extermination of people they deemed mentally and emotionally unfit. He said the world was faced with a population explosion, sooner or later policy makers would have to decide who would be given scare resources and allowed to survive and who would not, and as smart, educated, highly-ethical, scientifically-minded students they were going to be asked to help develop the criteria for making that decision.

Of the 570, 90 percent agreed that some people were more fit for survival than others. 89 percent suggested a painless drug be used to execute the unfit. 79 percent preferred one person to decide and another person to carry out the executions. 64 percent wanted the executioner to be anonymous. 29 percent supported the "final solution," even if it had to be applied to their own families.[48]

One of the clearest illustrations of how ordinary people can be made to engage in a terrible evil such as the "final solution" is the case of Reserve Battalion 101. In March 1942 80 percent of the victims of the holocaust were still alive. In February 1943, 80 percent were dead. With the help of the death squads from Reserve Battalion 101.[49]

Reserve Battalion 101 were a reserve unit from Hamburg, made up of elderly men, from lower-middle-class and working-class backgrounds, with no military experience, too old to be drafted by the army. The task they were assigned was the total extermination of all Jews in rural villages in Poland. To begin with 50 percent of the men refused. And police reservists killed the Jews they captured. But after a while they were persuaded to "do their bit." And by the end 90 percent of the unit were personally involved in the shootings of Jews. In just four months they shot to death 38,000 Jews at point blank range.[50]

47. Zimbardo, *The Lucifer Effect*, 274.

48. Ibid., 275.

49. Ibid., 285.

50. Ibid., 286.

Daniel Goldberg said anti-Semitism influenced "Hitler's willing executioners." But Philip Zimbardo says that anti-Semitism was not nearly as significant as authoritarianism.[51]

John Steiner (who had been a prisoner at Auschwitz) interviewed hundreds of SS about their involvement. He said, "it has become evident that not everyone playing a brutal role has to have sadistic traits of character." There were the "cruel" ones who enjoyed the killing, the "tough but fair" who "played by the rules," and the "good guards," who refused to join in the killing and who did small favors for Jews. (Steiner's own life was saved by SS personnel on several occasions.) He found that "these men lived normal—violence-free—lives before and after their violent years."[52]

"The trouble with Eichmann," according to Hannah Arendt, "was precisely that there were so many like him, neither perverted or sadistic, that were and still are, terribly and terrifyingly normal. His attitude towards wife and children, mother and father, brothers, sisters and friends was 'not only normal but most desirable.'"[53] And Hannah Arendt said, "Eichmann remembered that he would have had a bad conscience only if he had not done what he was ordered to do—ship millions of men, women, and children to their death with great zeal and the most meticulous care."[54]

C. P Snow says, "When you think of the long and gloomy history of [humanity], you will find far more hideous crimes have been committed [by both Christians and Muslims] in the name of obedience than have been committed in the name of rebellion."[55]

## Spiritual Perspectives—The Devil, Illusion, Desire, Ethos and Dogmatic Theology

There are four different types of spiritual perspectives, which seek to explain the relationship between the world of the spirit and the world of matter, and the particular matter of the atrocities, committed in the name of religion, that we are considering.

51. Ibid., 287.

52. Ibid., 286–87.

53. Ibid., 276.

54. Ibid., 288.

55. Ibid., 273.

~&~

The first spiritual perspective is the "traditional perspective." This perspective sees reality in terms of two parallel dimensions, a "heavenly" one and an "earthly" one, which intersect and interact and simultaneously reflect and reinforce the actions of one in the other.

From the traditional perspective, the atrocities we are contemplating could be seen—as they are, by Frank Peretti in his best-selling novels, *This Present Darkness* and *Piercing the Darkness*—as earthly skirmishes in a heavenly war between God and the devil.[56]

Certainly people like Martin Luther and John Calvin saw their battles precisely in these terms. Martin Luther said that "we are all subject to the devil."[57] And John Calvin said that the task of every saint is to engage in "unceasing struggle against the devil."[58]

In Islam the devil or Satan is known as *Iblīs* or *Shayṭān*. In Islam *Iblis* or *Shaytan* is a *jinn* (or genie) who has the power to cast evil suggestions into the hearts of men, women, and jinn.[59] In Iran, the USA and occasionally the UK have been referred to as the "Great Satan" because they have been viewed as spreading great evil around the world.[60]

So from this traditional perspective, people with blood on their hands may simply put their hands up and say that the Devil made them do it!

~&~

The second spiritual perspective is the "spiritualistic perspective." This perspective sees reality in terms of two parallel dimensions, a heavenly one that is manifest in the soul, and an earthly one that is manifest in the body. The heavenly dimension is "real" and "right," while the earthly dimension is either "unreal" or "wrong."

From the spiritualistic perspective, the atrocities we are contemplating could be seen, as they are by Baba Ram Das in his cult classic, *Be Here Now*, as nothing but a "bad dream" from which we will eventually "awake"

56. Peretti, *This Present Darkness*, and *Piercing the Darkness*.

57. Levack, *The Witch-Hunt*, 97.

58. Ibid., 97.

59. *Quran* 7:27

60. Buck, *Religious Myths and Visions of America*, 136.

to the realization that "pleasure and pain, loss and gain, fame and shame, are all the same—they're just happening."[61]

Certainly many Sufi Muslims and gnostic Christians see matters precisely in these terms. According to the Sufis, the "Only Ultimate Reality is God"—all else is illusion. This doctrine is called *wahdat al-wujud*.[62] According to the gnostics enlightenment will dispel the ignorance that has produced a nightmarish existence and experiences of terror.[63]

So from this spiritualistic perspective, people may say that transient things, like suffering, don't really matter one way or another in the light of eternity.

❧

The third spiritual perspective is the materialistic perspective. The materialistic perspective is the exact opposite of the spiritualistic perspective. It sees reality in terms of two parallel dimensions, an earthly one that is manifest in the body, and a heavenly one that is manifest in the soul. The earthly dimension is "real" and "right," while the heavenly dimension is either "unreal" or "wrong."

From the materialistic perspective, the atrocities we are contemplating could be seen, as they are by Sigmund Freud in his famous text on *The Future of an Illusion*, as nothing but "fulfillments of the oldest, strongest and most urgent wishes of mankind."[64]

Certainly people like Karl Marx and Friedrich Engels saw the issues precisely in these terms. They said that the so-called "religious" character of many of these Christian and Muslim activities was "simply a sacred cloak to hide desires that are very secular."[65]

So from this materialistic perspective, people may think that while religion isn't true, it is a powerful tool to mobilize the masses, because the masses believe it is true.

61. Alpert, *Be Here Now*, 107.

62. "Sufism: The Mystical Side of Islam." Online: http://www.rim.org/muslim/sufism.htm

63. Ellerbe, *The Dark Side of Christian History*, 12.

64. Freud, *The Future of an Illusion*, 30.

65. Marx, "Debates on Freedom of the Press" In *Early Texts*, 35.

The fourth type of spiritual perspective is the integral perspective. This perspective sees reality in terms of two coterminous aspects of the universe, an "outer" or "earthly" one, and an "inner" or "heavenly" one, so that every event has both an "outer," visible, material aspect and an "inner," invisible, spiritual aspect.

From the integral perspective, the atrocities we are contemplating, could be seen—as they are, by Morton Kelsey, in his beautiful book *The Other Side of Silence*—as material expressions of spiritual realities "that are actually parts of a single realm, [though] at present, they may appear to separate."[66]

Certainly people like Walter Wink and Charles Elliott see the events precisely in these terms. Walter Wink says, "institutions have an actual spiritual ethos and we neglect this aspect of institutional life to our peril."[67] Charles Elliott says, "we have to return to the basic position that [spiritual] powers control structures, and it is those powers that have to be confronted if the structures are to be set free" from their destructive proclivities.[68]

So from this integral perspective, people may say, if the spirit of a religion is compassionate and merciful, the more devoted the adherents are, the more compassionate and merciful their structures, agencies, and activities will be; but if the spirit of a religion is unsympathetic and pitiless, the more devoted the adherents are, the more unsympathetic and pitiless their structures, agencies, and activities will be.

Why would Christians and Muslims continue to commit such grievous crimes against humanity, as regularly as they do? Well, I think that the personal, political, and spiritual explanations that we have explored so far, do answer that question to a certain extent.

It is clear that Christians and Muslims capitulate to terrible personal and political evil. Many are part of authoritarian societies. Some develop authoritarian personalities themselves. Others are seduced by an intoxicating

---

66. Kelsey, *The Other Side of Silence*, 147.

67. Wink, *Engaging the Powers*, 6.

68. Elliott, *Comfortable Compassion*, 153.

cocktail of fear and avarice and power or are coerced by an overwhelming combination of hysteria and charisma and sanctions.

But why, you may well ask, don't their religions, which are meant to vouchsafe virtue, save them from succumbing *en masse* all too often to the "forces of darkness"?

One answer is, as we have seen, that it is all an illusion. A narrative, "full of sound and fury, signifying nothing." Now this answer is really a non-answer. If it is true, it doesn't really matter. Nothing really matters. It only really matters if it isn't true. And it isn't true. The suffering of millions of innocent people really matters.

Another answer is that religion is just an excuse pious people use to justify otherwise unjustifiable actions. The "Official" List of Religious Excuses includes: "The Lord told me to do it!" and/or "The devil made me do it!" Now this answer—at least the second bit of it—may be, at best, half the truth. But it is certainly not anywhere near the whole truth.

Last, but not least, is the answer to the question that religious people want to avoid at all costs: that the construction of their religion is not merely an excuse, but actually the real reason, that so many Christians and Muslims act in such a disgraceful manner.

Any suggestion that the religion we are devoted to is the *reason* that so many Christians and Muslims act in such a disgraceful manner, at a quick cursory glance might be considered by most devoted Christians and Muslims, to be heresy, even blasphemy.

But, as I take the stand, I put my hand on the Bible, I cross my heart, and I swear that: "It is the truth, the whole truth, and nothing but the truth. So help me God." Let me explain.

## A Closed Set Perspective of Religion and the Inevitable Problem of Violence

There are two completely different paradigms that Christians and Muslims (and others), have used through the centuries to understand their relationship to their religion—the "closed set perspective of religion" and the "open set perspective of religion." The most influential perspective is the "closed set perspective."

According to the "closed set perspective," a "set" is defined by its "enclosure." The very nature of the set is not "open" but "closed." From this perspective, a set of people who claim to have some connection to a religion can be shown to be part of the set by ascertaining whether their beliefs and behaviors are within certain set boundaries.

People who subscribe to a certain set of circumscribed beliefs and behaviors are "in." They are "insiders." People who don't subscribe to a certain set of circumscribed beliefs and behaviors are "out." They are not "insiders," but "outsiders." If an outsider is outside the set, but wants to become an insider, the only way for them to do so is by "opting in" to the set on the set terms. If an outsider finds him- or herself temporarily inside the set for some reason or other, but doesn't want to become a permanent insider by opting in to the set on the set's terms, they will typically find themselves criticized, frowned-upon, cold-shouldered and ostracized or "put out."

It is through defending these boundaries of belief and behavior that religious people define their religious identity. Hence Christians and Muslims have tended to fight to not only to *define* but also *defend* these boundaries of belief and behavior to the death, because not only their religious identity, but also their eternal destiny, depends on it.

There are certain obvious advantages that this "closed set perspective" affords. It is simple, precise, and portable; clear, concise, and communicable. The "unconverted" know what they have to do to be "saved," and the "converted" know what they have to do to "save" others. And when everyone has done what they know has to be done, everyone can be sure they are "saved." It is dream come true for proselytizers—be they soapbox preachers, street-corner pamphleteers, TV evangelists or tele-mullahs.

But there are numerous serious disadvantages of the "closed set perspective." Sure it is straightforward, but it is also superficial. It is essentially static: unchanging and unchangeable. It is a homogeneous ideology that admits no questions. Unless, of course, it asks and answers the questions itself. It is a uniform theology that demands complete conformity. There is no room at all for diversity, dissent, or disagreement. It is reductionist. It reduces a relationship to God to a formula of dogmatic theology. It is exclusive. It excludes anyone who cannot affirm the construction of the formula.

Is it violent? Not necessarily. But normally. For three reasons. One: Christians and Muslims tend to defend their boundaries to the death. Two: the best form of defense has always been attack. And, three: there are plenty of competing groups fighting for the right to define and defend their boundaries of belief and behavior for themselves.

Thus the "closed set perspective" rips the heart out of religion—replacing the warm, kind-hearted compassion of God with cold, hard-headed propositions about God; and relating to people in terms of an ideology of religion, rather than the mercy of God.

~☙~

Paul Hiebert, Professor of Anthropology at Fuller Theological Seminary, raised the alarm in 1978 about the dangerous implications of what he called, "bounded set" religion, in his seminal article on "Conversion, Culture, and Cognitive Categories."[69]

"What happens," Hiebert asks, "if we define our 'religion' in terms of a 'Bounded Set'?" Firstly, we tend to distort the meaning of what it means to be a Christian or a Muslim. Being a Christian or a Muslim is essentially a matter of the heart. But because we cannot see into the hearts of people, we make a working definition based on what we can see or hear—namely tests of orthodoxy (right beliefs) or orthopraxy (right behavior). So we can end up inadvertently making our working definition of religion, essentially a heartless one!

Secondly, we tend to distort our understanding of the relationship between Christians, and Muslims. The two categories of people are sharply differentiated. Because to have an unclear boundary is to undermine the very concept of a Christian (or a Muslim) itself. So, we have one set of people who are Christians who, by definition, are "not Muslims"; and another set of people who are "Muslims," who, by definition, are "not Christians." There is no place for anyone in between. Not even God. Because "there is no place in between"; only a boundary—a well-defined, well-defended, boundary.[70]

The theologian Robert Brinsmead comments on the very serious consequences of maintaining the boundaries Paul Hiebert talks about. A closed set perspective of religion:`

> draws lines of demarcation through the human race. The chosen people are distinguished from the unchosen, insiders from outsiders, clean from unclean, believers from unbelievers, the enlightened from the unenlightened. People who live within separate barriers cannot effectively communicate. What is orthodoxy to one group, is blasphemy to other, and vice versa. Each religion produces an elite that regards itself as superior to the rest of

69. Hiebert, "Conversion, Culture, and Cognitive Categories."
70. Ibid., 26–27.

humanity by virtue of possessing the truth. Such arrogance breeds estrangement and, eventually, hostility. Concrete examples of the ill-treatment of humanity, which inevitably follows such a devotion to religion are legion![71]

People committed to "closed set" religion have constantly been shown to be dogmatic[72] and judgmental[73] and, consequently, quite intolerant of political dissent.[74] They have constantly been shown to be more egocentric,[75] more ethnocentric,[76] and more uncharitable towards disreputable minorities than their nonreligious compatriots.[77]

The more popular a "closed set" religion becomes, the less likely they have been to champion important unpopular campaigns, like a due regard for universal basic human rights.[78] Once it has become established, it has typically been totally unwilling to advocate crucial anti-establishment causes, like liberty, equality, and democracy for all.[79]

Brinsmead begs Christians and Muslims to recognize it is religious devotees, such as ourselves, devoted to our mutually exclusive, inevitably conflictual, collision-bound bounded sets, that are directly, or indirectly, "moving millions towards a [global militant] *jihad* of violence everywhere," from Ireland to Lebanon, from Bosnia to India![80]

## An Open Set Perspective of Religion and the Credible Prospect of Nonviolence

Certainly there are many Christians and Muslims who would be horrified to realize just how much the language of the closed set perspective can, and does, embody violence towards anybody outside the boundaries of the bounded set. But unfortunately, it is so.

---

71. Brinsmead, *The Two Sources of Morality and Religion*, 5–7.

72. Rokeach, *The Open and Closed Mind.*

73. Wright, *Psychology and Moral Behaviour.*

74. Stouffer, *Communism, Conformity and Civil Liberties.*

75. Ellul, *The Ethics of Freedom*, 88–90.

76. Allport and Kramer, "Some Roots of Prejudice."

77. Glew-Crouch, *Religion and Helping Behaviour.*

78. Stellaway, "Religion," in *Christian Perspectives in Sociology*, 54.

79. Ibid., 255.

80. Ibid., 7.

If we want it to be otherwise, we need to find another way of defining our faith that is not so defensive; another way of affirming our faith that is not so aggressive; a way of comprehending our faith that is true, but doesn't pretend to have a monopoly on truth; and a way of interpreting our faith that is inclusive, not exclusive, of all that is good and healthy and holy and right in other cultures, traditions, and religions. And we can only do that, if we set aside a "closed set" perspective and embrace an "open set" perspective.

The open set perspective is the opposite of the closed set perspective. According to the closed set perspective, a "set" is defined by an enclosure circumscribed by the "experts." According to the open set perspective, a "set" is defined by a center, which is "free," and "cannot ever be confined or enclosed," least of all by the "experts."

From this perspective, a set of people who have a connection to God, show they are part of the set, not simply by choosing to subscribe to a certain set of beliefs and behaviors within certain set boundaries, but by choosing to overcome any boundary of belief or behavior that might prevent them from moving towards the compassionate spirit of God, exemplified in *Isa* and the *Bismillah*, which they have made the center of their lives.

The essence of closed set religion is all about defining and defending our religion. The essence of open set religion is all about becoming more open to God and encouraging everyone to become more open to God. Conversion for Christians and Muslims within a closed set perspective may mean confessing the creed or the *kalimah*. Conversion for Christians and Muslims seen from an open set perspective means constantly turning and moving towards the compassionate spirit of God, exemplified in *Isa* and the *Bismillah*, whether we use that language or not, judging our lives, for ourselves, in the light of God's love, and beginning to trust His love, to sustain us, on the journey of the greater *jihad* of personal growth and the lesser *jihad* of social change that He is calling us to be involved with.

There are some obvious disadvantages associated with the open set perspective. What you see depends on where you stand. So different groups tend to see different disadvantages. On the one hand, some of my Muslim friends might say, "Oh no. Not *Isa* again. It sounds too much like Christianity to me. Won't you Christians ever give up trying to take over the world, one way or another!" On the other hand, some of my Christians friends might say, "Oh no. It's not really very Christian. Sure, there are Christian words. But there are Muslim words too. What's all this about the *Bismillah*? I thought you were a Christian. Have you decided to become a Muslim?"

I must admit, it can get quite confusing. Which brings us to the major disadvantage of the open set, as compared to the closed set. With a closed perspective it is easy to judge where people stand in relation to the set, who is "in" and who is "out," etc. Whereas with an open set perspective it is difficult, if not impossible, for anyone, to judge whether anyone, except themselves, is "in" or "out" because everyone in an open set is moving towards the center from a different angle, a different distance, and a different direction; and those who may be "in" according to a closed set perspective, may be "out"; and those who maybe "out" according to a closed set perspective, may be "in."

But there are numerous significant advantages of the open set perspective. The first advantage is that it is centered. Stanley Jones, the famous inter-faith evangelist, says, "Get the center right, and the circumference takes care of itself."[81] The second advantage is that it is centered on *Isa* and the *Bismillah*, what Jones calls "the Best to which all Good points."[82] The third advantage is that as we move towards the center, we can move beyond the religions that divide us. *Isa* calls us to recognize the *Bismillah* embodied in other people of other religions. Jones says:

> John said to Jesus: "Master, we saw a man casting out demons in your name, but we stopped him because he is not a follower of ours." Jesus said to him "Do not stop him; he who is not against you is for you" (Luke 9:49–50). John tried to make "in your name" and "a follower of ours" synonymous. We still do that. Jesus showed the difference. "He who is not against you is for you." Whether Christian or Muslim.[83]

The fourth advantage is that as we move towards the center, we can move towards the One who can unite us as human beings made in the image of God.

> And behold, one came up to [Jesus] saying, "Teacher, which is the greatest commandment?" And Jesus said, "'Hear, O Israel, the Lord our God, the Lord is One. And you shall love the Lord your God with all your heart, with all your soul, with all your mind, and with all your strength.' This is the first commandment. And the second,

81. Jones, *The Way*, 59.

82. Ibid., 57.

83. Ibid., 56.

like it, is this: 'You shall love your neighbor as yourself.' There is no other commandment greater than these." (Mark 12:29–31)

And on this "common word" all Christians and Muslims and Jews can agree.

◆

On the Occasion of the *Eid al-Fitr al-Mubarak,* October 13th 2007, a gathering of a wide range of Muslim leaders from a broad range of Muslim groups, organizations, and denominations wrote an open letter to leaders of Christian churches, everywhere. In this open letter they said:

> Muslims and Christians together make up well over half of the world's population. Without peace and justice between these two religious communities, there can be no meaningful peace in the world. The future of the world depends on peace between Muslims and Christians.
>
> The basis for this peace and understanding already exists. It is part of the very foundational principles of both faiths: love of the One God, and love of the neighbor. These principles are found over and over again in the sacred texts of Islam and Christianity.
>
> The Unity of God, the necessity of love for Him, and the necessity of love of the neighbor is thus the common ground between Islam and Christianity.
>
> The following are only a few examples:
>
> Of God's Unity, God says in the Holy Qur'an:
>
> *Say: He is God, the One! / God, the Self-Sufficient Besought of all! (Al-Ikhlas,* 112:1–2).
>
> Of the necessity of love for God, God says in the Holy Qur'an:
>
> *So invoke the Name of thy Lord and devote thyself to Him with a complete devotion (Al-Muzzammil,* 73:8).
>
> Of the necessity of love for neighbor, the Prophet Muhammad said: "*None of you has faith until you love for your neighbor what you love for yourself.*"
>
> In the New Testament, Jesus Christ said: "*'Hear, O Israel, the Lord our God, the Lord is One. / and you shall love the Lord your God with all your heart, with all your soul, with all your mind, and with all your strength.' This is the first commandment. / and the second, like it, is this: 'You shall love your neighbor as yourself.' There is no other commandment greater than these.*" (Mark 12:29–31)
>
> In the Holy Qur'an, God Most High enjoins Muslims to issue the following call to Christians (and Jews—the *People of the*

*Scripture):* Say: O People of the Scripture! Come to a common word between us and you: that we shall worship none but God, and that we shall ascribe no partner unto Him, and that none of us shall take others for lords beside God. And if they turn away, then say: Bear witness that we are they who have surrendered (unto Him). (Aal 'Imran 3:64)

The words: *we shall ascribe no partner unto Him* relate to the Unity of God, and the words: *worship none but God,* relate to being totally devoted to God. Hence they all relate to the *First and Greatest Commandment.* According to one of the oldest and most authoritative commentaries on the Holy Qur'an the words: *that none of us shall take others for lords beside God,* mean "that none of us should obey the other in disobedience to what God has commanded." This relates to the Second Commandment because justice and freedom of religion are a crucial part of love of the neighbor.

Thus in obedience to the Holy Qur'an, we as Muslims invite Christians to come together with us on the basis of what is common to us, which is also what is most essential to our faith and practice: the *Two Commandments* of love.

*In the Name of God, the Compassionate, the Merciful, and may peace and blessings be upon the Prophet Muhammad.*[84]

What an invitation! This is an invitation that no sincere person should reject. Our Muslim brothers and sisters are calling Christians to practice what we preach: to practice that law of God written on our hearts—the love of God and the love of neighbor—which Jesus said was the "greatest commandment"—together.

It is only in this spirit that we can overcome our "not-so-holy" so-called "Holy Wars."

---

84. "A Common Word Between Us and You. An Open Letter." (2007). Online: http://www.acommonword.com/

# PART TWO

## The *Jihad* of *Isa*

According to Khalid Muhammad Khalid, Jesus or *Isa* "was his message. *He was the supreme example he left. He was the love which knows no hatred, the peace which knows no restlessness, the salvation which knows no perishing.*"[1]

Ahmad Shawqi says: "*kindness, chivalry and humility were born the day Jesus was born. His coming brightened the world, his light illuminated it. Like the light of the dawn flowing through the universe, so did the sign of Jesus flow. He filled the world with light, making the earth shine with its brightness. No threat, no tyranny, no revenge, no sword, no raids, no bloodshed did he use to call to the new faith.*"[2]

The crucifixion of Christ presents people with a choice. "At that time they had a well-known prisoner whose name was Jesus Barabbas. So when the crowd had gathered, Pilate asked them, 'Which one do you want me to release to you: Jesus Barabbas [an extremist], or Jesus who is called the Christ?'" (Matt 27:16–18). Khalid Muhammad Khalid says "*The Spirit of Barabbas glorifies force, violence and tyranny. With Muhammad, the faithful, we declare 'Christ not Barabbas, the true not the false, love not hatred, peace not war, life not extinction.'*"[3]

---

1. Khalid, *Ma'an 'ala-l-Tariq*, 188–89.

2. Shawqi, *Al-Shawqiyyat*, 12.

3. Khalid, *Ma'an 'ala-l-Tariq*, 52.

# 4

## Reframing *Jihad* as a Method
## of Nonviolent Struggle

### The Normal Healthy Human Being
### Is a Conscientious Objector

Some people believe that violence is inevitable and so nonviolence is not credible. But I've just been reading a book called *On Killing*. It's a study about killing in combat. It's not written by a pacifist propagandist, but by a military paratrooper psychologist, who goes by the name of Lieutenant Colonel Dave Grossman.[1] And Grossman cites research that suggests— contrary to some of our most famous cultural stereotypes—"the vast majority of men are *not* born killers."[2] At most only 2 percent of men could be considered aggressive psychopathic personalities with a predisposition towards killing.[3] A figure reflected in the kill figures of fighter pilots in World War II, where only 1 percent of fighter pilots accounted for more than 40 percent of all enemy planes shot down.[4]

Grossman quotes Brigadier S. L. A. Marshall, whose study of soldiers' conduct in World War II suggests "that the average healthy individual has such a resistance towards killing a fellow man that he will not of his own

---

1. Grossman, *On Killing*.
2. Ibid., 31.
3. Ibid., 189.
4. Ibid., 110.

volition take life if it is possible to turn away from that responsibility."[5] A view that is reflected in the shots-per-soldier and the kills-per-shot recorded in every major war from the American Civil War through to World War I up until World War II. During this period, when it became possible to measure shots fired in combat, research has showed that the vast majority of soldiers—between 75 percent and 95 percent—either did not fire their weapon (even when fired upon) or only fired into the air, refusing to kill the enemy, even when given orders to do so.[6]

In American Civil War times, conscience-stricken soldiers had the option of pretending to fire—that is, loading up their muskets, mimicking the movements of a firing soldier next to them, and pretending to recoil. These soldiers would then be carrying loaded weapons or would have loaded their weapons multiple times.

When the fighting at Gettysburg was over, 27,574 muskets were found on the battlefield. Over 90 percent were loaded. Given that loading a weapon took roughly twenty times as long as firing it, the chances of these muskets representing mostly soldiers cut down just as they intended to shoot are slim. But then how do you explain the 12,000 multiply-loaded weapons, with 6,000 of them loaded with 3–10 rounds apiece? The most obvious answer is these soldiers could not fire their weapons. "Most soldiers were trying not to kill the enemy. Most appear to have not wanted to fire in the enemy's general direction."[7]

The Battle of Gettysburg is considered one of America's bloodiest battles, but as Grossman shows, it could have been a great deal bloodier. Averages and estimates suggest that during Napoleonic and Civil War times, an entire regiment, firing from a range of thirty yards, would hit only one or two men a minute.

Let's break down the numbers. A regiment contains between 200 and 1,000 men. A soldier operating at peak efficiency could get off between one and five shots per minute. During training, these soldiers were 25 percent accurate at 225 yards, 40 percent accurate at 150 yards, and 60 percent accurate at 70 yards. So, taking the most modest of these estimates—a 200 man regiment shooting once per minute with 25 percent accuracy—you would expect to see about fifty hits, which would be more than twenty-five times greater than that which actually happened.

5. Ibid., 1.
6. Ibid., 3.
7. Ibid., 23.

As one officer observed, "It seems strange that a company of men can fire volley after volley at a like number of men at not over a distance of fifteen steps and not cause a single casualty. Yet such were the facts in this instance."[8] What was happening? Soldiers were resorting to a range of options that meant that they didn't have to kill. Some fell back to support positions. A few faked injury or ran away. Many fired into the air.

Colonel Milton Mater's uncle said the most significant fact he could remember about his combat experience in the World War I was "draftees who wouldn't shoot."[9]

Gwynne Dyer says that apart from "the occasional psychopath who really wants to slice people open" most soldiers on both sides of World War II were interested in "damage limitation."[10] And "all forces had somewhere near the same rate of non-firers."[11]

According to Brigadier Marshall, "At the vital point [when a soldier has to decide to fire or not] the normal healthy human being *becomes a conscientious objector.*"[12]

## How Soldiers Are Systematically Socially Conditioned as Killers

When the military realized what was happening, they embarked on a new program to turn their soldiers into killers. They knew that while they couldn't change the vast majority of men's natural aversion to killing, they could put soldiers under sustained systematic pressure to kill—by framing killing as saving lives, portraying the enemy as sub-human, increasing the distance between the trigger and the target so soldiers cannot see the humanity of the enemy, demanding every soldier's immediate obedience to the commands of their leader and developing each unit's capacity for collective violence.

8. Ibid., 20.
9. Ibid., 29.
10. Ibid., 6.
11. Ibid., 16.
12. Ibid., 1.

## 1. Framing killing as saving lives

As it has become clear that most men are motivated to serve and to preserve life, the military has taken the desire to serve and preserve life and used it to make men killers by telling men that killing is the only way they can the save the lives of those they love. Soldiers in Iraq, for instance, are told killing terrorists is the only way to save the lives of civilians.

## 2. Portraying the enemy as sub-human

In World War II it became clear that soldiers found it harder to kill people they could identify with, but easier to kill people they couldn't identify with. Only 6 percent of Americans said they wanted to kill Germans; while 44 percent said they wanted to kill the Japanese.[13] So the military has encouraged soldiers to see the enemy in Iraq as "rag-heads" rather than humans.[14] As it has become clear it is harder for soldiers to kill people who are innocent; but easier to kill people who are guilty; "rag-heads" are deemed bloodthirsty baby killers in advance.[15]

## 3. Demanding every soldier's obedience to their leader

Sigmund Freud said "never underestimate the power of the need to obey."[16] Those with no combat experience presume that being fired upon was the reason most soldiers fired. But veterans of combat say that being ordered to fire was the reason most soldiers fired.[17] Without an order to fire many soldiers would not fire, even when they came face to face with the enemy in combat.[18]

Gwynne Dyer said in his book on *War* that while "the vast majority of men are not born killers" nonetheless "men will kill under compulsion— men will do almost anything if they know it is expected of them and they are under strong social pressure to comply."[19]

13. Ibid., 162.
14. Ibid., 161.
15. Ibid., 165.
16. Ibid., 142.
17. Ibid., 143.
18. Ibid., 144.
19. Ibid., 31.

Since Marshall's report on surprisingly low firing rates, the military have tried to increase soldiers' compliance with orders to fire through social learning, classical conditioning, and operant conditioning. Through social learning, men have been socialized to imitate role models like the ANZAC legends who obeyed orders to attack impregnable positions in Gallipoli—even when it was obvious to everyone that the orders were insane and to obey them was suicidal.[20] Through the classical conditioning[21] devised by Pavlov to make dogs salivate at the sound of a bell,[22] soldiers have been conditioned to associate obeying the orders of drill sergeants[23] with rewards (pleasure), and disobeying orders with punishment (pain).[24] And through behavioral engineering,[25] devised by Skinner to make rats go through mazes,[26] soldiers have been engineered to increase their automatic quick-shoot reflex[27] by repeatedly shooting at targets that look like people in simulated battlefield conditions[28] to such a degree that an average infantryman now has a 95 percent shot-per-soldier rate[29] and a marksmen now has a 1.39 shot-per-kill ratio.[30]

## 4. Developing each unit's capacity for collective violence

Research has shown that the greatest fear a man has in combat is not fear of death but of "letting others down."[31] "You can't turn around and run the other way. Peer pressure, you know?"[32] So the military have used peer pressure—along with the intensification of power[33] and the diffusion of

20. Ibid., 306.
21. Ibid., 255.
22. Ibid., 254.
23. Ibid., 322.
24. Ibid., 255.
25. Ibid., 255.
26. Ibid., 255.
27. Ibid., 256.
28. Ibid., 256.
29. Ibid., 36.
30. Ibid., 256.
31. Ibid., 52.
32. Ibid., 150.
33. Ibid., 151.

responsibility that a group provides[34] ("there were so many guys firing, you can never be sure it was you" who killed someone[35])—to turn men into killers. Konrad Lorenz says: "Man is not a killer, but the group is."[36]

Grossman concludes his book *On Killing* by saying that the same techniques used by the military are now being used by the media in society at large—and that not only soldiers, but also civilians, are being socialized to kill without constraints by watching movie heroes kill outside the constraints of the law;[37] being desensitized to the act of killing by seeing thousands of people being killing on television;[38] and being engineered to kill reflexively by shooting at human targets with model guns in life-like video games.[39]

## 5. Increasing the distance between the trigger and the target

Most soldiers find it difficult to kill up close and personal. "Where you hear 'em scream and see 'em die, it's a bitch."[40] It has always been easier to kill from a distance and to pretend it's not personal. Sailors shoot up "ships." Aviators shoot down "planes."[41] The artillery attack enemy "lines."[42] "They can pretend they are not killing human beings."[43]

So the military is increasing the distance between the trigger and the target technologically as quickly as it can. Through night goggles, for example, when a soldier shoots someone they say it's just like shooting on a TV show "as if it's happening on a TV screen."[44]

34. Ibid., 152.
35. Ibid., 111.
36. Ibid., 151.
37. Ibid., 325.
38. Ibid., 329.
39. Ibid., 319.
40. Ibid., 117.
41. Ibid., 58.
42. Ibid., 58.
43. Ibid., 108.
44. Ibid., 170.

## How Terrorists Are Systematically
## Socially Conditioned as Killers

Extremist organizations, like *Jemaah Islamiyah* (JI) use many of the same approaches to create terrorists. JI, which has been proscribed as a terrorist organization, is based in Indonesia, Malaysia, Singapore, and the Philippines.[45] Members of JI participated in the war in Afghanistan with the *Mujahideen* against the Russians in the 80s. Many members of JI met members of *al-Qaeda* and were inspired by Osama Bin Laden's "*fatwa* made on 22 Feb 1998 that urged Muslims to kill Americans, its allies and destroy its interests."

Their "extreme violent ideology is carried out through the pro bombing faction of JI [that used to be] under the leadership of Nordin Mohd Top."[46]

An extremist organization like *Jemaah Islamiyah* is of particular interest to me as an Australian, as JI organized the bombings in the district of Kuta on the Indonesian island of Bali, which killed 202 people, including eighty-eight Australians, and wounded a further 240.[47]

The Religious Rehabilitation Group (RRG)—a local Singaporean group of *Ulama* (religious scholars) and *Asatizah* (religious teachers) "who volunteer their services to counsel detainees to assist them in understanding their religion correctly"—have studied how JI use a distorted construct of Islam to socially condition their members as killers. They acknowledge "there are various factors that plunge one into terrorism, yet, for the JI, ideology, and not other factors, is the source and main motivation for the terrorists."[48]

RRG say "there are [five] steps towards becoming a terrorist or adopting a terrorist worldview." The first step is Introduction to JI. The second step is cultivation in the JI ideology "through [a] thought reforming process which will change a person's way of looking at the world." The third step is initiation into the JI community, "to secure one's commitment through rites

---

45. Religious Rehabilitation Group, "Our Message." In R.R.G. (Singapore, 2014). Online: http://www.rrg.sg/index.php?option=com_content&view=article&id=15%3Aour-message&catid=2%3Aour-message&Itemid=6&limitstart=1

46. Ibid., 2.

47. "Suicide Bomber Praying as He Detonates Bomb: Survivor." *The Jakarta Globe*, April 15, 2011. Online: http://thejakartaglobe.beritasatu.com/archive/suicide-bomber-praying-as-he-detonates-bomb-survivor/435595/

48. Religious Rehabilitation Group, 6.

and oaths as official process of recruitment (as 'One of us')." The fourth step involves integration into the JI agency, which includes "de-individuation" (renunciation of individual identity) and "diffusion of responsibility" (resignation of personal responsibility) so there is projection of moral responsibility of a particular plan onto the group. And the fifth step is recruitment into the JI agenda of terrorist activity, which is operationalized by "obeying their legitimate [that is, legitimate to JI] authority."[49]

Like the military, JI systematically socially condition recruits by:

## 1. Framing killing as saving lives

As it has become clear that most men are motivated to serve and to preserve life, JI have taken the desire to serve and preserve life and used it to make men killers, by telling men the only way they can the save the lives of those they love is by re-establishing an exclusive closed-set *Daulah Islamiyah* or Islamic State, and the only way to re-establish a *Daulah Islamiyah* or Islamic State is by killing all those "infidels" who get in the way.[50]

## 2. Portraying the enemy as sub-human

As it has become clear that people find it easier to kill people they don't identify with, groups like JI have consistently labeled "all those who do not adhere to their agenda" to establish a *Daulah Islamiyah* or Islamic State, as *takfir*. "Even though it is forbidden in Islam to pronounce anyone as an 'infidel'" JI condemns all Muslims they disagree with as "not real Muslims." Designating "not real Muslims" as apostates not only gives JI recruits "a legal loophole around the prohibition of killing another Muslim," but also turns that prohibition into "a religious obligation to execute" these apostates.[51]

## 3. Demanding every recruit's obedience to their leader

Initiation into JI is "through rites and oaths" to secure one's commitment to obedience.[52] As Gwynne Dyer said in his book on *War*, while "the vast

---

49. Ibid., 1.

50. Ibid., 3.

51. Eikmeier, "Qutbism," 85–98.

52. Religious Rehabilitation Group, 6.

majority of men are not born killers [nonetheless] men will kill under . . .
a strong social pressure to comply."[53] That pressure to comply in JI is based
on their call for recruits to be committed above all else to *Al-Wala'* or total
loyalty to God, His Prophet and Their Amirs (i.e., Their JI leaders).

## 4. Developing each unit's capacity for collective violence

Research has shown that the greatest fear of a man in combat is not the fear
of death but of "letting others down" or peer pressure.[54] So JI have used peer
pressure. Integration into JI includes de-individuation (renunciation of individual identity) and diffusion of responsibility (resignation of personal
responsibility)[55] so there is projection of moral responsibility of a particular
plan onto the group. "Man is not a killer, but the group is."[56]

## 5. Decreasing the distance between the guts and the glory

One of the biggest differences between terrorists and soldiers is this: most
soldiers find it difficult to kill up close and personal, but terrorists can kill
up close and personal with courage, conviction, and determination. That is
because JI indoctrinates its recruits with the ideology that for Muslims to be
"true Muslims" they need to destroy *jahiliyyah*—the "state of ignorance"—
through a *jihad*, defined as a "resolute, offensive, violent struggle," which
demands *syahadah* or martyrdom through *istimata* or suicide bombing.[57]

## From a Closed Set Islamic Ideology
## to an Open Set Islamic Theology

As a distorted Islamic ideology undergirds terrorist groups, like JI, RRG
says we need to challenge "their twisted form of Islamic concepts which
forms their ideology of terror."[58]

---

53. Dyer, *War*, 31.
54. Grossman, *On Killing*, 150.
55. Religious Rehabilitation Group, 1.
56. Grossman, *On Killing*, 151.
57. Religious Rehabilitation Group, 2.
58. Ibid., 6.

It is interesting to note, though the words are different, the ideas that undergird some Christian extremist groups are similar to the ideas that undergird Muslim extremist groups. Hard (as distinct from Soft) dominionism, developed from Calvinist Christian Reconstructionism, advocates that Christians take dominion over the world, impose their view of biblical law on the whole population, under which "error has no rights," where "sinners" do not have "the right to life" (as "the wages of sin is death") and the list of civil crimes which carry a death sentence would include homosexuality, adultery, lying about one's virginity, idolatry, apostasy, public blasphemy and false prophesying.[59]

These extremist ideas may seem far out and far off, but I can remember not so long ago being called in to discuss these matters with a committee appointed by the synod of a church in my own home state. I was greeted at the door, and shown a chair at the end of a table, around which were seated a set of some of the most seriously dressed men I had ever seen. When we were all seated, a very somber looking man, at the head of the table, announced he would select a passage from the Bible to set the scene for our discussion. He picked up the big old book on the table in front of him, and, in a deep stentorian voice, began to read:

> In the cities of the nations, the Lord your God is giving you as an inheritance: Do not leave anything that breathes alive! Completely destroy them—the Hittites, the Amorites, the Canaanites, the Perizzites, the Hivites and the Jebusites—as the Lord your God has commanded you!

Then, the somber man closed the book, and said, "So you can see, that in the Bible there is no such thing as 'inalienable human rights.' God's people are simply called to do God's will," he said—with a cold, hard, matter-of-fact finality—"*whether that is to cure, or to kill!*"

I could hardly believe my ears. Here I was, in downtown Brisbane, the capital of peaceful sunny Queensland—"beautiful one day, perfect the next"—and I was listening to a well-regarded Christian leader justifying wholesale slaughter in the name of God!

The equivalent Muslim concepts that RRG says we need to challenge, deconstruct, and reconstruct are the idea of re-establishing an exclusive closed-set *Daulah Islamiyah* or Islamic State, the idea that all those who do not adhere to their agenda to establish a *Daulah Islamiyah* or Islamic

---

59. Durand, "Reconstructionism's Commitment to Mosaic Penology."

State are *takfir*, the idea that *al-wala wal bara* means allegiance to "us," no allegiance to "them," and *bai'ah*, their pledge of allegiance, means a commitment to absolute obedience to their *Amir* (leader), the idea that *jihad* means war, and the coming of Islam means the execution and elimination of all non-Muslims.[60]

Now, there is no better place to begin that process of deconstruction and reconstruction of a closed set Islamic ideology than with an open set Islamic theology of the *Bismillah*.

The *Bismillah* stands for the Arabic phrase *Bismillah ir-Rahman ir-Rahim*, a poetic phrase my Muslim friends say contains the true essence of the *Qur'an*, indeed the true essence of all religions. Every chapter of the *Qur'an* (except the ninth chapter) begins with this phrase, which is most commonly translated, "In the name of God, most Gracious, most Compassionate." And my Muslim friends begin everything they do with the *Bismillah*.

*Bismillah* or *bismi Allah* means "in the name of Allah." "Allah" is not the Muslim name for God, still less the name of a Muslim God, but the Arabic name of the One True God. The Semitic roots of the word *Allah* extend back thousands of years to the Canaanite *Elat*, Hebrew *El* and *Elohim*, and Aramaic *Alaha*. To recite the *Bismillah* is to recall there are not many gods but One God and that One God is not Muslim or Christian, but the One whom we belong to and who belongs to us all, whether Muslim or Christian or Jew.[61]

Both *rahman* and *rahim* are derived from the Semitic root *rhm*, which "indicates something of the utmost tenderness and kindness which provides protection and nourishment" from which the creation is brought into being. The root *rhm* has meanings of *womb, nourishing-tenderness, loving-kindness*. According to Ibn Qayyum (1350 AD), *rahman* describes the quality of limitless grace with which God embraces the whole of the world and all of those who dwell in it, while *rahim* describes the general embracing grace of God as it interacts with us in the particular circumstances of our lives, always proactive, always prevenient, always responsive.[62]

Nora Amath, from AMARAH (the Australian Muslim Advocates for the Rights of All Humanity), says that

---

60. Religious Rehabilitation Group, 6.

61. "Bismillah al rahman al Rahim.", http://wahiduddin.net/words/bismillah.htm

62. Ibid.

God opens almost every chapter of the *Qur'an* with those very words: *"Ar-Rahmaan, Ar-Rahiim,"* most commonly translated as "The Most Compassionate, The Most Merciful." As Muslims, we need to deeply reflect on the significance of this, because out of His 99 Most Glorious Attributes, these are the 2 that God refers to Himself the most in His Revelation. *"He is the Lord of mercy, the Giver of mercy"* (Quran 59: 22). There are many verses in the *Qur'an* where Allah (SWT) emphasizes this: *"My mercy encompasses all."* (Quran 7:156)"

Nora says "in one of the traditions, the Prophet Muhammad states: *'Those who have no mercy on other human beings will not receive the mercy of God.'* She says "it is important to note that in this *hadith* the word used is *nas*, that is people, not just Muslims or believers of Islam." She says "Abdullah bin Umro bin Aas, reports that the Prophet (SWS) said: *'Have mercy on those who are on earth, the One in heaven will have mercy on you (Tirmidhi).'"* She says that "the mercy needs to extend to all *'those who are on earth.'"*

How can we interpret our sacred texts of our religions in a way that reflects a radical spirituality of compassion? We invited our Muslim friends to share with us the way they go about it. They said,

> Every *sura* in the *Qur'an* except one, begins with *"Bismillahi ir Rahman ir Rahim—In the name of God the most Gracious and most Compassionate."* And we have come to believe we should use that invocation as a hermeneutic to interpret the text in the light of the Spirit. Thus to interpret the text in the light of the Spirit of God, all our interpretations must be consistent with the grace and compassion of God.

When my Muslim friends told me they believe they need to interpret the *Qur'an* according to the *Bismillah*, in the light of the amazing grace and compassion of God, even if it contradicts a human interpretation of *sharia* law, I jumped for joy. "That's wonderful!" I said. "I think what you are doing is great. I think Jesus would think what you are doing is great too; because he did exactly the same as what you are doing with the *Qur'an* with the *Torah*; including being willing to challenge closed set human interpretations of the Law in the light of God's open set grace and compassion."

Maulana Wahiduddin Khan says "God is Peace or *As-Salam*." He says "the very word '*Islam*' (from the Arabic *silm*) means 'peace.' So, according to the Prophet, peace is a prerequisite of Islam." He says *"a Muslim is one from whose hands people are safe.*"[63] Oh, that this were true, for all Muslims, Christians, and Jews. And I believe it can be true if we allow ourselves to be born again in the spirit of the *Bismillah,* inhaling the *Bismillah* with every breath, and embodying the *Bismillah* with every beat of our heart, through every vein in our head, and our hands, and our feet. *"Bismillah ir-Rahman ir-Rahim!"*

## Reconstructing an Ideology of Jihad
## in Terms of a Theology of the *Bismillah*

As we have noted the *Bismillah* stands for the Arabic phrase *Bismillah ir-Rahman ir-Rahim,* commonly translated, "In the name of God, most Gracious, most Compassionate." According to Ibn Qayyum, *rahman* describes the quality of limitless grace with which God embraces the whole of the world and all of those who dwell in it, while *rahim* describes the general embracing grace of God as it interacts with us in the particular circumstances of our lives, always proactive, always prevenient, always responsive.[64]

In the light of the *Bismillah,* it is not surprising that Maulana Wahiduddin Khan says, "a truly Islamic movement arises out of feelings of benevolence for all humanity."[65] He says "The *Qur'an* begins not with a diatribe (with implied criticism of wrong governance) but simply with praises to God (in the *Bismillah*). And it ends with the necessity to seek refuge in God." He says, "In the *Qur'an* and the *Hadith,* there is no mention of the system of state,"[66] and no "political interpretation of Islam, which offer[s] Muslims the status of God's vice-regents on earth, with the right to rule the entire world on His behalf."[67]

Maulana Wahiduddin Khan blames Jamaluddin Afghani, Sayyed Qutb, and Sayyed Abdul Ala Maudid for developing and disseminating the idea of establishing or re-establishing a closed-set *Daulah Islamiyah* or Islamic State, exclusively by Muslims for Muslims. But most of all Maulana Wahiduddin Khan blames the *Dajjal,* the "great deceiver," working behind the scenes, using the language of Islam to promote anti-Islamic ideas, all

---

63. Khan, *The Prophet of Peace,* xi.
64. "Bismillah al rahman al Rahim."
65. Khan, *The Prophet of Peace,* 41.
66. Ibid., 41–42.
67. Ibid., 37.

the while "convincing the people that what he offers is the true version of Islam."[68]

Maulana Wahiduddin Kahn says the *Dajjal's* particularly diabolical form of evil (*fitna*) is

> projecting Islam not just as a religion but also as a political sys-
> tem. According to this modern political interpretation of Islam,
> it should be the duty of believers to bring to an end the rule of
> non-Islamic law all over the world and replac[e] it with the rule of
> Islamic law. In other words, the sole aim of Muslims is to raise the
> political flag of Islam; they are duty bound to conquer non-Islamic
> communities and establish the dominance of Islam; the aim of
> *jihad* is to establish this universal Islamic government.[69]

Maulana Wahiduddin Kahn says "this ideology is without doubt, the greatest evil (*fitna*) of modern times. The greatest harm it does is to eternally divide the inhabitants of this earth into two warring groups. One group will fight to gain power, while the other will fight to save itself from being subjugated."[70] Maulana Wahiduddin Kahn says "this version of Islam, focused on political thinking, is almost bereft of God-orientated thinking."[71] What he calls the "the political *ghulu* has overridden all the human quali-ties that qualify a community for honor and glory—[like] benevolence, universality, acknowledgment of others, looking at all human beings as God's family, fostering the *dawa* spirit, giving importance to the values of peace."[72] He says "it engages in political confrontation, it has no sympathy for human beings, seeing others only as rivals, so that they cannot be seen as friends. It breeds a jungle of hatred, not an orchard of love."[73]

Maulana Wahiduddin Kahn says "the preacher, who has nothing but benevolence in his heart, exhorts his listeners to accept a way which is peaceful, non-political and non-violent."[74] And preachers with that be-nevolence include Sardar, Tibi, and Bencheikh.

---

68. Ibid., 157.

69. Ibid., 158. Maulana Whahiduddin Khan is not advocating a modern sacred/secu-lar split but a personal-moral/political-imperial distinction.

70. Ibid., 158.

71. Ibid., 161.

72. Ibid., 53.

73. Ibid., 161.

74. Ibid., 158.

Ziauddin Sardar, asserts that "the equation of Islam with the state" is a "catastrophe." Sardar accuses Islamism of reducing Islam to a "totalitarian" ideology that leads to a "totalitarian state." "The transformation of Islam into a state-based political ideology deprives it of all ethical content and debunks most Muslim history as un-Islamic."[75]

Bassam Tibi, argues for a separation of religion and politics. Religion should be about faith and ethics. Politics should be about the government and governance. What Islam needs are "religious reforms maintaining the spirit but [aiding] its depoliticization."[76]

Soheib Bencheikh, the Grand Mufti of Marseille, says that unlike Islamists who dream of establishing Islamic states, with a theology of "a majority faith" Muslims in most of the world need to learn to develop "a minority faith that does not impose itself by force."[77]

Separating religion from politics does not mean we do not bring our faith and the ethics derived from our faith to bear on our politics in terms of our discussions about policies. To the contrary, all real believers cannot help but bring their faith and the ethics derived from their faith to bear on their politics in terms of our ethical discussions about policies. But separating religion from politics means not using our particular religion for party political purposes as a means of manipulation or exploitation to gain or retain power.

For our faith to be "non-political" means for it to be "non-partisan" and "not-imposed."

◦

As we have noted *Bismillah* or *bismi Allah* means "in the name of Allah," which is not the Muslim name for God, still less the name of a Muslim God, but the Arabic name of the One True God. And for us to recite the *Bismillah* is to recall there are not many gods but One God and that One God is not a Muslim or Christian or Jew, but the One whom we belong to and who belongs to us all, whether we are Muslim or Christian or Jew, etc.[78]

75. Sardar, "Rethinking Islam."

76. Tibi, *Islam between Culture and Politics*, 271, 266.

77. Bencheikh, "Islam and Secularism."

78. "Bismillah al rahman al Rahim." Online: http://wahiduddin.net/words/bismillah. htm

In the light of the *Bismillah,* it makes sense, Maulana Wahiduddin Khan says, that

> God has the same compassionate relationship with every man as a father has with all his children. Therefore it is alien to the divine scheme of creation that this earthly plane should be marred by hatred and violence. It is God's most cherished desire that love should be returned for hatred and violence should be met with peace. According to the *Qur'an,* paradise is God's neighborhood and in this neighborhood only those who have compassion, living in a way [their] actions are of benefit to others, find acceptance.[79]

Farid Esack says Muslims frame their relationships to others in terms of *iman* and *kufr,* usually translated as "belief" and "unbelief." He says that originally these terms were seen as "qualities that individuals may have" but as Islamic theology became more rigid these terms were "no longer seen as qualities [of] individuals" but "qualities of groups."[80]

According to the *Qur'an* the term *iman* and its noun, *mu'minun,* are defined as follows:

> *Indeed the* mu'minum *are only those whose hearts tremble whenever God's name is mentioned; and whose* iman *is strengthened whenever His* ayat *[signs] are conveyed unto them; and who place trust in their Sustainer. Those who are constant in prayer and spend on others what We provide for them as sustenance. It is they who are truly the* mu'minum. *(8:2–4)*

Esack says three interconnected themes may be discerned from this text: "the dynamic nature of *iman*" (to be "attained"), "*iman* as a personal response to God," ("hearts tremble with awe when God is mentioned") and the "interrelatedness of *iman* and righteous deeds" ("spend on others out of what [God] provide[s] for them as sustenance").[81]

Esack says, given the fact that *iman* requires righteous deeds, it cannot be attained simply by "the practice of rituals" and "given the fact that *iman* is a deeply personal response to God," it "cannot be confined to a particular socio-religious community." He says "such attempts would be a denial of the universality of God. This is why the *Qur'an* is explicit about the *iman* of those outside the socio-religious community of the *mu'minum.*"[82]

79. Khan, *The Prophet of Peace,* 16.

80. Esack, *Qur'an, Liberation and Pluralism,* 114–15.

81. Ibid., 118.

82. Ibid., 125.

Esack says we need to see *islam* as verb rather than a noun. He quotes Toll who says: "primordial and universal *islam*, i.e., that is, the attitude of surrender to the Absolute in co-fraternity, can be discerningly discovered and acknowledged in the most varied patterns of belief and action, in the religions and ideologies of the past and present."[83]

That there are people, of other religions and of other ideologies, which may be very different from Muslim traditions, who may serve God in the same way sincere Muslims do, is made very clear in the *Qur'an* when it says:

> *Not all of them are alike; among them is a group who stand for the right and keep nights reciting the words of Allah and prostrate them-selves in adoration before Him. They have faith in Allah and in the Last Day; they enjoin what is good and forbid what is wrong, and vie with one another in good deeds. And these are among the righteous.*
> (4:113)

According to the *Qur'an* there is only one "*din*" ("religion"), but there are many a "*ummah*" ("community"), and God has sent to each different "*ummah*" ("community") a different guide with a different "*shir'ah*" ("path") and "*minhaj*" ("way") to the "*tawhid*" (the "Oneness of God"). The same *din "was enjoined on Noah, Abraham, Moses, and Jesus"* as on Muhammad (42:13). "*For every* ummah *there is a messenger*" (10:47) and "*unto every one of you We have appointed a* [different] shir'ah [path] *and* minhaj [way]."(5:48) [84]

It is important to note while the *Qur'an* frequently associates *iman* with the followers of Mohammad (fifty-five times), it often associates *iman* with the followers of Moses (eleven times), and associates *iman* with the followers of many other prophets too (twenty-two times).[85]

The *Qur'an* says "*To every community We have appointed acts of devotion, which they observe; so let them not dispute with you in the matter . . .*" (22.67). So why the disputes?

In spite of the *Qur'anic* call to recognize unity in diversity and respect diversity in unity, the reality is that "the tension in the religious-ideological relationships between the Muslims and the People of the Book (i.e. Jews and Christians) was inevitable."[86] Each of these groups, contrary *Qur'anic* advice about not getting involved in disputes, set themselves up as guardians

83. Troll, "The Qur'anic View of Other Religions: Grounds for Living Together."

84. Esack, *Qur'an, Liberation and Pluralism*, 166.

85. Ibid., 118.

86. Ibid., 151.

of their sacred texts, defined and defended their interpretations in terms of separate, competing, and conflicting closed set religions, denounced those who disagreed with their interpretations of their sacred texts as *kufr* and declared "not-so holy" so-called "Holy War" on one another to prove their superiority in the disputes.

In the *Qur'an* the word *kufr* stands for the "rejected other," and the notion of the "rejected other" concerns one "who reject[s] the signs of God," and is not a chauvinistic or xenophobic exclusion of "the other."

The *Qur'an* says

> *Verily as for those who are reject/ungrateful (yakfur) for the signs of God, and slay the Prophets against all right and slay those people who enjoin justice, announce unto them grievous chastisement. It is they whose works shall come to naught both in this world and in the life to come, and they shall have none to succor them.* (3:21–2)[87]

There are number things we need to note in this passage—first, it is talking about an active attitude of an individual (or collection of individuals) not an ethno-socio-religious group; second, that the attitude identified is not of one who is simply an other believer, an unbeliever, or an infidel, but one who is completely ungrateful, totally rejects the grace of God and violently lashes out against the prophets—not only Muhammad, but also Moses and Jesus and others—and attacks everything they taught about grace; and third, that the "grievous chastisement" to be visited upon them

---

87. This passage reminds me of a story Jesus told in the Gospels: "There was a rich man who was dressed in purple and fine linen and who feasted sumptuously every day. And at his gate lay a poor man named Lazarus, covered with sores, who longed to satisfy his hunger with what fell from the rich man's table; even the dogs would come and lick his sores. The poor man died and was carried away by the angels to be with Abraham. The rich man also died and was buried. In Hades, where he was being tormented, he looked up and saw Abraham far away with Lazarus by his side. He called out, 'Father Abraham, have mercy on me, and send Lazarus to dip the tip of his finger in water and cool my tongue; for I am in agony in these flames.' But Abraham said, 'Child, remember that during your lifetime you received your good things, and Lazarus in like manner evil things; but now he is comforted here, and you are in agony. Besides all this, between you and us a great chasm has been fixed, so that those who might want to pass from here to you cannot do so, and no one can cross from there to us.' He said, 'Then, father, I beg you to send him to my father's house—for I have five brothers—that he may warn them, so that they will not also come into this place of torment.' Abraham replied, 'They have Moses and the prophets; they should listen to them.' He said, 'No, father Abraham; but if someone goes to them from the dead, they will repent.' He said to him, 'If they do not listen to Moses and the prophets, neither will they be convinced even if someone rises from the dead.'" (Luke 16:19–31.)

(on the Day of Judgment, by God) is to be announced by believers, not to be visited upon them by the believers.[88]

Sure, this passage raises serious issues about the making of judgments, about the Day of Judgment, and about the idea of rewards and punishments meted out by God. But we will have to save those conversations for another time. For now, suffice it to say, as Maulana Wahiduddin Khan says, "In all the chapters of the *Qur'an,* with their hundreds of verses, there is not a single verse which gives the command to kill an abuser of the Prophet."[89]

～

As we have noted, Maulana Wahiduddin Khan says, "God is Peace or *As-Salam.*" He says "the very word *Islam* (from the Arabic *silm*) means peace." So, "according to the Prophet, peace is a prerequisite of Islam." He says "*a Muslim is one from whose hands people are safe.*"[90] And this could be true, for all Muslims and Christians and Jews, if all Muslims and Christians and Jews would only allow themselves to be born again in the spirit of the *Bismillah,* inhaling the *Bismillah* with every breath and embodying the *Bismillah* with every beat of our heart through every vein in our head and our hands and our feet.

In the light of the *Bismillah,* Abdul Ghaffar Khan says, we need to remember that if we do have conflict with one another, the "weapon of the Prophet" we should use is *sabr* or "patience." "*If you exercise patience, victory will be yours. No power on earth can stand against it.*" He says we need to be mindful that the *Qur'an* says,

> there is no compulsion in religion; forgive and be indulgent; render not vain your almsgiving by injury; whosoever kills one—for other than manslaughter—it shall be as if he had killed all mankind, and whoso saves the life of one, it shall be as if he had saved the life of all mankind.[91]

This is, of course, completely contrary to the idea *al-wala wal bara* which means allegiance to "us," no allegiance to "them," and for Muslims to be "true" Muslims they would need to destroy *jahiliyyah* (the "state of

88. Esack, *Qur'an, Liberation and Pluralism,* 134.
89. Khan, *The Prophet of Peace,* 207.
90. Ibid., xi.
91. Easwaren, *A Man to Match His Mountains,* 117, 209.

ignorance") through a *jihad* characterized as a "resolute, offensive, violent struggle"[92] (which will demand *syahadah* or martyrdom through *istimata* or suicide bombing) [93] to eliminate everything non-Muslim from society.[94]

In his classic book *Reconstructing Jihad amid Competing International Norms*, Halim Rane argues we need to wrest the concept of *jihad* from the control of the extremists and deconstruct and reconstruct our interpretation of *jihad* in the light of the *Qur'an*.

Rane says if we are to interpret the *Qur'an* correctly, each verse needs to be interpreted in terms of the text, the language, the meaning it had for the people at the time it was written, and the meaning it has for people reading it in today's world, in the light of the *Bismillah*, in the context of the *maqasid* or "overall general objective" of *Islam*.[95]

Quoting Kamali, Rane says the *maqasid* or overall general objective of *Islam* is based "in textual injunctions of the *Qur'an* and the *Sunnah*" that he says, quoting Raysuni, are focused on "wisdom, mercy, justice, and equity" and directed to "the benefit of mankind," which, quoting Qaradawi, he says, includes "welfare, freedom, dignity, and fraternity."[96]

One verse that needs to be carefully (re)interpreted—in terms of the text, the language, the meaning it had for the people at the time it was written, and the meaning it has for people reading it in today's world, in the light of the *Bismillah*, in the context of the *maqasid* of *Islam,* the general objective of wisdom, mercy, justice and equity—is the (in)famous "sword verse" which instructs Muslims to slay Christians: ordering them *"to slay those who ascribe divinity to aught but God, wherever you may come upon them"* (9:5).[97]

Rane says "this verse along with Quran 9:29 (which says *'fight those from among the People of the Book who believe neither in God, nor in the Last Day, nor hold as unlawful what God and his Messenger have declared to be unlawful, nor follow the true religion, until they . . . agree to submit'*) has been quoted throughout Muslim history to justify aggression and aggressive wars against non-Muslims because of their 'unbelief.'" Rane says, "as noted by *al Qaeda* expert Abdel Bari Atwan these verses are among those

92. Qutb, *Milestones*, 63–69.

93. Religious Rehabilitation Group, 2.

94. Qutb, *Milestones*, 130, 134.

95. Rane, *Reconstructing Jihad amid Competing International Norms*, 165.

96. Ibid., 168–70.

97. Ibid., 186.

most commonly quoted by *al Qaeda* leaders and published on the Internet for recruitment."[98]

> Asad explains that this verse should be read in conjunction with those that precede it. (In 9:5 it says "*As for those who have honored the treaty you made with them, and have not supported anyone against you: fulfill your agreement with them to the end of their term. God loves those who are righteous.*") Of central importance is that these verses were revealed in the context of "warfare already in progress with people who [had] become guilty of a breach of treaty obligation and of aggression." That non-Muslims are to be fought because of their unbelief rather than their act of aggression is doubtful given that verse 9:5 continues "*if they repent, and take to prayer regularly and pay alms, then let them go their way. God is forgiving and merciful*" and verse 9:6 commands the Muslims to give protection and security to those among the enemy who seek it. If their unbelief was the basis of fighting against them, this provision would be nonsensical.[99]

Rane says "in the context of conflict, the pursuit of peace is paramount to the extent that the *Qur'an* instructs Muslims; *'Do not allow your oaths in the name of God to become an obstacle to virtue and God-consciousness and the promotion of peace between people'* (2:224). Peace should not be rejected, even from a non-Muslim encountered in war (4:94)."[100]

Like the Maulana who says, "God is Peace or *As-Salam,*" and "the very word *Islam* (from the Arabic *silm*) means peace," Rane insists peace, not war, is the purpose of *Islam*, and *jihad* is the path to peace. Rane asserts that in the *Qur'an* the word for "war" is not *jihad,* but *qital,* and that the word *jihad* means "struggle," not "war." He says that there 6,000 verses in the *Qur'an,* and out of those 6,000 verses, only thirty-five verses refer to *jihad;* and out of those thirty-five verses, twenty times *jihad* is used ambiguously, eleven times *jihad* is used unambiguously in terms of peace, and four times *jihad* is used unambiguously in terms of war.[101]

Where the word *jihad* is used ambiguously or unambiguously in the context of war, Rane says, the *Qur'an* imposes strict "rules of engagement" to temper the use of violence with "wisdom, mercy, justice, and equity" in the hope of minimizing "force, suffering, ignominy, and enmity" and

98. Ibid., 186.
99. Ibid., 186–87.
100. Ibid., 193.
101. Ibid., 141–42.

maximizing "welfare, freedom, dignity, and fraternity." Rane says that according to the *Qur'an*, the conduct of *jihad* in war would need to take eight rules for engagement into account. One, killing—except in self-defense—is considered a grievous sin.[102] Two, war is only permitted for self-defense and self-determination.[103] Three, all wars of aggression are forbidden.[104] Four, if you are not specifically attacked by enemies you should not to attack them, even if they are your enemies.[105] Five, Muslims should never ever use difference of religion with non-Muslims as an excuse for a war of aggression.[106] Six, in war, Muslims should protect all places of worship, not only mosques, but also churches and synagogues.[107] Seven, in war, Muslims should protect "helpless men, women and children,"[108] "even the accidental harm of the innocent is a 'grievous wrong' for which those responsible are guilty."[109] Eight, if peace is offered by your attacker, it should not be rejected, even if the sincerity of the offer is dubious, as God always wants his people to "give peace a chance."[110]

Similarly, in Christianity, Ambrose and Augustine developed a set of criteria to call those in power—who make war—to temper the use of violence with "wisdom, mercy, justice, and equity." They argued that in order for a war to be conducted according to the principles of justice it would need to meet eight specific conditions. One, it would need to be motivated by a just cause—and the only cause considered to be just was to stop the killing of large numbers of people. Two, it would need to be administered by a just authority—duly constituted authorities had to proceed carefully according to due process before taking action. Three, it would always need to be a last resort—after all means of negotiation, mediation, arbitration, and nonviolent sanctions had been exhausted. Four, it would need to be for a just purpose—to secure the welfare, safety, and security of all parties in the dispute, including the enemy. Five, it would need to be a reasonable risk—not a futile gesture, but a realistic venture, with a reasonable hope

102. Ibid., 178.
103. Ibid., 178.
104. Ibid., 181.
105. Ibid., 190.
106. Ibid., 184.
107. Ibid., 179.
108. Ibid., 183.
109. Ibid., 189.
110. Ibid., 193.

of success. Six, it would need to be cost effective—the outcomes of victory would outweigh the human costs of battle. Seven, that any government intending to go to war should announce their intentions—articulating the conditions that would need to be met to avert it—in order to avoid going to war if at all possible. Eight, that, if the war were to go ahead, that not only the ends, but also the means would need to be just—noncombatants must be protected; once combatants surrender, they too must be protected from slaughter; and all prisoners must be protected from torture.

According to these criteria, none of our current wars are "just wars," they are just "wars."

If we are to struggle for justice with integrity, dignity, and grace we need to reject all the calls to a violent *jihad* of "not-so-holy" so-called "Holy Wars" and embrace the nonviolent *jihad* of the "whole-hearted strong-but-gentle struggle for justice against injustice."

Qader Muheideen (Chaiwat Satha-Anand) says "the purpose of *jihad* ultimately is to put an end to 'structural violence,'"[111] and we must choose means consistent with that end. Muheideen says for *jihadists* to end violence we have to choose nonviolent means.[112] He says there are eight cogent Islamic reasons to reframe *jihad* as a nonviolent struggle:

1. For Islam, the problem of violence is an integral part of the Islamic moral sphere.

2. Any violence used must be governed by the rules of engagement in the *Qur'an*.

3. If any violence used in modern warfare and/or terror campaigns cannot discriminate between combatants and noncombatants, it is quite unacceptable to Islam.

4. Modern technologies of destruction, used in modern warfare and/or terror campaigns, like drones and bombs, render discrimination virtually impossible.

5. So in the modern world, fighting today's battles, Muslims cannot use violence.

6. Islam teaches Muslims to fight for justice against injustice in the light of the truth that human lives are genuinely sacred and taking human lives is a grievous sin.

111. Satha-Anand, "The Nonviolent Crescent," 10.
112. Ibid., 11.

7. In order to be true to Islam, Muslims must use nonviolent strategies and tactics in the struggle, such as submission to the will of Allah and nonviolent civil disobedience.

8. Islam is a strong resource for a nonviolent struggle because of its tradition of personal discipline, social responsibility, robust perseverance, and self-sacrifice.[113]

Added to these philosophical/theological reasons are two practical/historical reasons:

9. The use of nonviolent means is more likely to bring about nonviolent ends, like a democratic society with accountable administration and unarmed opposition.[114]

10. And the use of nonviolent means and ends are more likely to get the support and approval of the international community "amid competing international norms."[115]

Rane says Islamic practices such as *salat* (prayer), *zakat* (charity), and *sawm* (fasting) are resources for the inner personal *jihad* and practices such as *hajj* (pilgrimage) and *hijra* (migration) provide processes for the outer social *jihad*, but it is *sabr* (patience) that provides the reserves for an ongoing struggle with integrity, dignity, and grace.[116]

113. Ibid., 23.
114. Chenoweth and Stephan, *Why Civil Resistance Works.*
115. Rane, *Reconstructing Jihad amid Competing International Norms*, 114–26.
116. Ibid., 123–24.

# 5

## Reclaiming Jesus as a Model
## of Nonviolent Struggle

### *Isa Masih*—"The Supreme Example"

Many conversations between Christians and Muslims about *Isa* or Jesus deteriorate from dialogue into debate and from debate into dispute, generating more heat than light on the subject. Often this occurs because both sides want to impose their own particular view of *Isa* or Jesus on the other and are unable and/or unwilling to respect the other person's particular point of view.

In order to avoid such unproductive disputations, I have written the following observations based on those views of *Isa* or Jesus that both the Qur'an and the *Injil* or the Gospel (as recorded in the Gospels in the New Testament, according to Matthew, Mark, Luke, and John) have in common.

While I acknowledge the significant differences Christians and Muslims have about *Isa*/Jesus, I have intentionally tried to focus on those beliefs about him that Christians and Muslims have *in common* as the place for us to *start* our conversations, treating "*common ground*" not as suspect compromise, but as "*sacred ground*" on which we can stand and speak to one another.

Mohamad Abdalla is regarded as one of Australia's most respected Muslim leaders, combining the roles of academic scholar and religious leader. He is Associate Professor and Founding Director of the Griffith Islamic Research Unit (GIRU) and the Director (QLD Node) of the National

Centre of Excellence for Islamic Studies Australia (NCEIS). Recently, in an introduction to a book I wrote on Jesus, or *Isa*, Mohamad Abdalla wrote:

> Muslims have always believed in the Prophet-hood of Jesus—or *Isa*—(peace be upon him) not due to political expediency but because it is an integral part of their faith. In fact, to reject Jesus, his Prophet-hood, or that he was born from a virgin mother is tantamount to disbelief. The *Qur'ān* (Islam's Holy Book) is replete with anecdotes about the life and teachings of Jesus including his miraculous birth; his noble teachings; the miracles he performed by God's permission; and speaks of him as a respected Prophet of God. Furthermore, the *Qur'ān* repeatedly reminds its readers that Jesus was a human being sent with the same message that other Prophets and Messengers were assigned to deliver: there is no god but God, who ought to be worshipped alone.
>
> It is profound, to say the least, that Islam is the only religion (other than Christianity) that recognizes Jesus and makes it compulsory upon its adherents to believe in him.[1]

Ahmad Shawqi records:

> kindness, chivalry and humility were born the day Jesus or Isa was born. In him, the Gospels or the Injil says, "was life and that life was the light of all humanity. The light shines in the darkness and the darkness has not overcome it"(John 1.4). . . . His coming brightened the world, his light illuminated it. Like the light of the dawn flowing through the universe, so did the sign of Jesus flow. He filled the world with light, making the earth shine with its brightness. No threat, no tyranny, no revenge, no sword, no raids, no bloodshed did he use to call to the new faith.[2]

However, the *Qur'an* says "O People of the Scripture! Do not exaggerate in your religion, and do not say about God except the truth. The *Masih*, *Isa*, the son of *Maryam*, is the Messenger of God" (4:171).

> And God will say, "O *Isa*, son of *Maryam*, did you say to the people, 'Take me and my mother as gods rather than God?'" He will say, "Glory be to You! It is not for me to say what I have no right to. Had I said it, You would have known it. You know what is in my soul. You are the Knower of the hidden. I only told them what You commanded me: that you shall worship God" (5:116–17)

1. Andrews, *Isa*, 11.

2. Shawqi, *Al-Shawquiyyat*, 12.

I am one of the "People of the Scripture," and I would say *the Scriptures are pretty clear. Isa never asked anyone to worship him. Jesus or Isa's preferred self-reference was not the "Son of God," but the "Son of Man."* Walter Wink says.

> "The Son of Man" is the expression Jesus almost exclusively used to describe himself. In Hebrew the phrase simply means "a human being." The implication seems to be that Jesus intentionally avoided honorific titles, and preferred to be known simply as "the man," or "the human being." He saw his task as helping people become more truly human.[3]

The Messiah or *Masih*, as the *Qur'an* says, "does not disdain to be a servant of God" (4:172) Jesus or *Isa*, in the Gospels or *Injil*, says "the Son of Man did not come to be served, but to serve, and to give his life as a ransom for many" (Mark 10:45). One time Jesus, or *Isa*, "poured water into a basin and wash[ed] his disciples' feet, drying them with the towel wrapped around him" (John 13:5).

Jesus, or *Isa*, the "Son of Man" said, *"'O God, our Lord, send down for us a table from heaven, to be a festival for us, for the first of us, and the last of us, and a sign from You.' God said, 'I will send it down to you'"* (5:114–15). Jesus, or *Isa*, said "go to the street corners and invite to the banquet anyone you find" (Matt 22:9). Jala al-din Rumi, in his Mathnawi, wrote: "The house of *Isa* was the banquet of men of heart. From all sides the people thronged. Many blind and lame, halt and afflicted, at the door of *Isa* at dawn, that with his breath he might heal their ailments. O afflicted one, quit not at the door."[4]

In the *Qur'an* God said *"We gave Isa miracles"* (2:253). *Isa* said, *"I heal the blind and the leprous, and I revive the dead, by God's leave"* (3:49). "News about him spread all over Syria, and people brought him all who were ill with various diseases, those suffering severe pain, those having seizures, the demon-possessed, the paralyzed; and he healed them" (Matt 4:24).

> He spoke, saying: "O stricken ones, the desires of your heart have been granted by God, arise, walk without pain and affliction." Then all, like camels, whose feet are shackled, when you loose their feet, rush [a]way in joy and delight.[5]

---

3. Wink, *The Human Being*, xi.

4. Whinfield, *Masnavi-i-Ma'navi: Spiritual Couplets*, 116.

5. Ibid., 116.

Jesus said, "whoever wants to save their life will lose it, but whoever loses their life for me and for the Gospel will save it" (Mark 8:35).

> God said "*We gave him [Isa] the Gospel, wherein is guidance for the righteous. So let the people of the Gospel rule according to what God revealed in it*" (5.46, 47). "*We gave him the Gospel, and instilled in the hearts of those who followed him compassion*" (57.27). Jesus, or Isa, was asked: "*Are there any like you?*" He answered: "*Yes. Whoever has prayer for his speech, meditation for his silence, and tears [of compassion] for his vision, he is like me.*"[6]

God says in the *Qur'an* "*whenever a messenger came to you with anything your souls do not desire, you grew arrogant, calling some impostors, and killing others*" (2:87). The Gospels (*Injil*) say of Jesus (*Isa*), "He came to his own, but his own did not receive him" (John 1:11). "In him was life, and that life was the light of all humanity" (John 1:4). "But people loved darkness instead of light, because their deeds were evil" (John 3:19). Even "*after the clear signs had come to them; they disputed*" (2:253). Even "*when he [the Masih] showed them the miracles, they said, 'This is obvious sorcery'*"(61:6).

"The *Qur'an* constantly presents what perhaps we can call the 'occupational hazard' of being a prophet."[7] People criticize them, people chastise them, and people "put them to death" (2:87). Being a prophet, *Isa* was no exception. But, for most Christians and Muslims "the crucifixion of *Isa*" is a point of contention. Many Christians say they "preach Christ crucified," cruelly killed on a cross (1 Cor 1:23), while many Muslims would say the Qur'an denies the crucifixion actually occurred. "*God will defend those who believe*" (22:49), and "*He confounds the plots of the enemies of Christ*" (3:54).

However, the issue of the crucifixion of Jesus/Isa is not as simple or dualistic as either/or. The *Qur'an* is more complex, paradoxical, and both/and than either side would like to believe. On the one hand, the *Qur'an* says "*God will defend those who believe*" (22:49); "*He confounds the plots of the enemies of Christ*" (3:54). On the other hand, "God says, '*O Isa, I am causing you to die and raising you to Myself*'" (3:55). On the one hand, the Jews say, "*We have killed the Christ, Isa*" (4:157). On the other hand, "*they did not kill him, nor did they crucify him, but it appeared as if they did*"(4:157).

How do we make sense of this? One possible interpretation that avoids the simplistic either/or and embraces the complex both/and of the text is that the *Qur'an* means: "*They* [the Jews] did not kill him, nor did they

6. Al-Ghazali, "The Sayings of Jesus," in *Ihya Ulum al-Din*, Book 4, Section 35.

7. Cragg, *Jesus and the Muslim*, 167.

crucify him[—the Romans did it]. But it appeared as if they did." Other possible interpretations are that the Jews did not kill him on the cross, but they were "under the illusion" that they did it (Abd al-Latif)—either because "they killed a man who looked like *Isa* but actually wasn't him" or because when Jesus/*Isa* was "actually taken down from the cross, life was still in him."[8]

Muhammad Kamil Husain says, "*The idea of a substitute for Christ is a very crude way of explaining the Qur'anic text. No cultured Muslim believes that nowadays.*"[9] Al-Baidawi opposed the idea that Christ "swooned" on the cross but survived. Instead, he suggested the possibility that "*God did actually allow [him] to die on the cross and to remain dead prior to his rapture into heaven.*"[10] After all, God says, "*O Isa, I am causing you to die and raising you to Myself*"(3:55), and Jesus/*Isa* says: "*Peace is upon me the day I was born, and the day I die, and the Day I get resurrected alive*"(19:33).

*Whatever our interpretation, the 'crucifixion of Christ' presents people with a choice.*

> At that time they had a well-known prisoner whose name was Jesus Barabbas. So when the crowd had gathered, Pilate asked them, "Which one do you want me to release to you: Jesus Barabbas [an extremist], or Jesus who is called the Christ?" (Matt 27:16–18)

Khalid Muhammad Khalid says "The Spirit of Barabbas glorifies force, violence and tyranny. With Muhammad, the faithful, we declare 'Christ not Barabbas, the true not the false, love not hatred, peace not war, life not extinction.'"[11]

In the *Ma'an 'ala-l-Tariq: Muhammad wa-i-Masih*, Khalid Muhammad Khalid says,

> Christ was himself his message. He was the supreme example he left. He was the love which knows no hatred, the peace which knows no restlessness, the salvation which knows no perishing. And when we (Christians and Muslims—together) realize all these things on this earth, we shall then comprehend the return of the Christ.[12]

---

8. Ibid., 172.

9. Husain, *City of Wrong*, 222.

10. Cragg, *Jesus and the Muslim*, 177.

11. Khalid, *Ma'an 'ala-l-Tariq*, 52.

12. Ibid., 52.

Shams Hafiz al-Din says, "And if the Holy [Spirit] descend, his comfort in these days to lend, to them that humbly wait on it, theirs too the wondrous works can be, that Jesus wrought in Galilee."[13]

## A Sicari-Carrying Kind of Zealotry?

Many Christians, Muslims, and Jews all use the retaliation advocated in the Hebrew Bible to justify their eye-for-an-eye reactive violence. After all, they say, Moses himself said, "if there is serious injury, you are to take life for life, eye for eye, tooth for tooth, hand for hand, foot for foot, burn for burn, wound for wound, bruise for bruise" (Exod 21:23–24).

Celebrity pastors like Mark Driscoll loudly and proudly proclaim that "Jesus is not a pansy or a pacifist. In Revelation, Jesus is a pride fighter with a tattoo down His leg, a sword in His hand and the commitment to make someone bleed. He is saddling up on a white horse, coming to slaughter His enemies and usher in his kingdom. Blood will flow." Driscoll says that a tough "eye-for-an-eye" guy "is a guy I can worship. I cannot worship a guy I can beat up."[14]

Driscoll is right to say Jesus was not a "pansy-passivist," but he is wrong to say Jesus was not a "pacifist." *Jesus was a compassionate activist who embodied the original model of nonviolent struggle for inspirational personal growth and transformational social change.*

How then do we explain Mark Driscoll's explicit biblical references to Jesus and swords and this view—supported by Reza Aslan, in his recent brilliant bestselling book *Zealot*—that they demonstrate Jesus was a zealous violent revolutionary who advocated the use of arms, such as swords, in order to "slaughter his enemies and usher in his kingdom"?[15]

According to Aslan "If one knew nothing about Jesus of Nazareth save that he was crucified by Rome, one would know practically all that was needed to uncover who he was, what he was, and why he ended up nailed to a cross." He says, "The purpose of crucifixion was not so much to kill the criminal as to serve as a deterrent to others who might defy the state." He insists Jesus was crucified as a *lestai* or a *rebel* "for sedition."[16]

13. Cragg, *Jesus and the Muslim*, 62.
14. Murray, "The God Who Bleeds."
15. Aslan, *Zealot*, 78.
16. Ibid., 155–58.

Aslan acknowledges Jesus was not a card-carrying Zealot—as the Zealot party only came into existence thirty years after his crucifixion—but writes that Jesus sympathized with the hidden-dagger *sicari*-carrying kind of zealotry that later produced the Zealot party.[17]

The argument Aslan advances is that "the Gospels, written forty years after his death, glossed over [Jesus'] violence with sweet-peace talk so that the early Christians wouldn't appear as political threat to the Romans."[18] But, he says, the evidence for characterizing Jesus as a zealous violent revolutionary is clear, cogent, and incontrovertible:

- Jesus criticized the authorities (Mark 10:42; Luke 13:32)

- He wanted to overthrow the status quo (Luke 6:19–22)

- He sought to establish an upside-down system (Mark 9:35)

- He drove the rip-off merchants out of the temple (John 2:15)

- He said that he came not to bring peace but a sword (Matt 10:34)

- And he asked his disciples to purchase swords themselves (Luke 22:36–38)[19]

This argument may seem plausible, as many of the facts alluded to are beyond dispute, but there are some very serious hermeneutical problems with this biblically-defective, politically-fanciful, and historically-inaccurate (mis-)representation of Jesus of Nazareth.[20]

## "No Sword, No Raids, No Bloodshed"

We need to look carefully at what Jesus actually said. He referred to "swords" specifically five times in the Gospels. On one occasion, Jesus said, "Do not think that I have come to bring peace to the earth; I have not come to bring peace, but a *sword*" (Matt 10:34). On another occasion, Jesus said to the disciples, "the one who has no *sword* must sell his cloak and buy one" (Luke 22:36). When the temple police came to arrest him, Jesus said, "Have you come out with *swords* and clubs as if I were a bandit?" (Luke 22:52). When Peter unsheathed his sword to protect Jesus, he said, "Put your *sword* back into its sheath" (John 18:11). Jesus final word on swords was: "*Put your*

17. Ibid., 41.

18. Kraybill, *The Upside-Down Kingdom*, 60.

19. Aslan, *Zealot*, 78.

20. Dixon, "How Reza Aslan's Jesus Is Giving History a Bad Name."

*sword back into its place; for all who take the sword will perish by the sword"* (Matt 26:52).

What are we to make of these statements? Even the disciples often had difficulty understanding many of his statements because, as a prophet, Jesus often used beautiful, unforgettable-but-metaphorical, poetic language to express his opinions, they frequently misinterpreted what he said because they took his metaphors too literally and he got frustrated with them because even after years they still didn't understand him.

For example,

> When they went across the lake, the disciples forgot to take *bread*. "Be careful," Jesus said to them. "Be on your guard against the *yeast* of the Pharisees and Sadducees." They discussed this among themselves and said, "It is because we didn't bring any *bread*." Aware of their discussion, Jesus asked, "You of little faith, why are you talking among yourselves about having no *bread*? Do you still not understand?" (Matt 16:5–9)

"Just because Jesus talked about *yeast*, that in a literal sense is used to make *bread*, doesn't mean he was talking literally about *bread*."[21] And, I would say, just because Jesus talked about a *sword*, that in a literal sense is used to shed *blood*, doesn't mean he was always talking literally about using a *sword* and the shedding of *blood*.

> When Jesus said "Do not suppose that I have come to bring peace to the earth, but a *sword*" (Matt. 10:34) it is clear by the context *he does not mean a physical sword* that cuts up and bloodies the family, but a *spiritual one that may divide it up non-physically*. And it is precisely Luke who clarifies Jesus' meaning of "sword" as *nonliteral,* in the two parallel passages of Matthew 10:34 and Luke 12:51. If Luke does this in 12:51, then why would he not shift slightly the meaning of "*sword*" in Luke 22:36–38?[22]

With this perspective in mind lets seek to intelligently interpret the text in which Jesus said to the disciples, "the one who has no *sword* must sell his cloak and buy one" (Luke 22:36). In context (Luke 22:35–38) the text reads:

> **35** Then Jesus asked them, "When I sent you without purse, bag or sandals, did you lack anything?" "Nothing," they answered. **36** He

---

21. Mooney, "The Problem with Interpreting Jesus' Words Literally."

22. Arlandson, "A Brief Explanation of the Sword in Luke 22:36."

said to them, "But now if you have a purse, take it, and also a bag; and if you don't have a *sword*, sell your cloak and buy one. **37** It is written: 'And he was numbered with the transgressors'; and I tell you that this must be fulfilled in me. Yes, what is written about me is reaching its fulfillment." **38** The disciples said, "See, Lord, here are two swords." "*That is enough*," he replied.

A literal interpretation of this text on the two swords is inadequate for two reasons.

First, the obvious question is: two swords are enough for what? Are they enough for a physical fight to resist arrest? This is hardly the case because during Jesus' arrest a disciple (Peter according to John 18:10) took out his sword and cut off the ear of the servant of the high priest. *Jesus sternly tells Peter to put away his sword, "No more of this!" and then he heals the servant, restoring his ear* (Luke 22:49–51). Resisting arrest cannot be the purpose of the two swords.

Second, were the two swords enough for an armed rebellion to resist the authorities and to impose the new Jesus movement in a political and military way? Jesus denounces this purpose in Luke 22:52, as the authorities are in the process of arresting him: "Am I leading a rebellion that you have come with swords and clubs?" The answer is no, as he is seized and led away (v. 54). So the physical interpretation of Luke 22:36 (the two swords were intended to be used) will not work in the larger context. *Two swords are not enough to resist arrest, let alone help them to pull off a revolt of some kind.*

More likely, in v. 38, when Jesus says, "*That is enough*," Jesus is saying, "enough of this conversation—you still are not understanding that I am speaking of spiritual things, not material." In other words, "*enough of this nonsense!*"[23]

*Jesus might say the same about anyone who would take these texts and interpret them literally to justify arming themselves with swords for armed resistance or rebellion!*[24]

23. "Answers to objections to Christian Pacifism." Plow Creek Mennonite Church. Online: http://www.plowcreek.org/answers.htm

24. Including anyone like Mark Driscoll who willfully takes the text in Revelation, in which it says the "sword" Jesus has "proceeds from his mouth" (Rev 19:21)—the "Sword of the Spirit" which is the "Word of God" (Eph 6:17). "For our struggle is not against enemies of blood and flesh, but against . . . the spiritual forces of evil in the heavenly places" (Eph 6:12).

A nonliteral ironical metaphorical reading of this text is much more adequate for two reasons. First, Jesus reminds the disciples of his mission for them before he arrived in Jerusalem (Luke 9:3; 10:1–17). Did they need a purse, a bag, or extra sandals? No, because people were friendlier, and their opposition to him was spread out over three years. Now, however, he is in Jerusalem, and he has undergone the compacted antagonism of religious leaders seeking to trap him with self-incriminating words. When the authorities are not present, they send their spies. The atmosphere is therefore tense, and *the two swords represent the tension—no more than that*. Jesus' mission has shifted to a clear danger, and the disciples must beware. *However, he certainly did not intend for his disciples to literally use the swords, as we just saw, for he is about to tell Peter to put away his sword.*

Second, their literal interpretation of his words and acquisition of two swords ironically means he will, as the Scripture says, be "numbered among the lawless" (Luke 22:37). By far the clearest purpose of the two swords is explained by Jesus' reference to Isaiah's prophecy (Isa 53:12). He was destined to be arrested like a criminal, put on trial like a criminal, and even crucified like a criminal. What are criminals known for carrying with them? Weapons, and *to be numbered among criminals, Jesus must also have weapons*. That is why he said that only two swords would be enough—to fulfill this prophecy.[25]

How ironic, that this man, known for his persistent opposition to violence, is arrested and charged because two of his twelve disciples were armed with two swords he never wanted!

We need to look carefully at what Jesus actually *did* and interpret what he actually *said* in terms of what he *did*. In the account of Jesus' arrest (Matt 26:51–52) one of Jesus' disciples reached for his *sword*, drew it out, and struck the servant of the high priest, cutting off his ear. "Put your sword back in its place," Jesus said to him, "for all who draw the sword will die by the sword." Then Jesus healed the servant, restoring his ear.

"When Jesus rebuked Peter," Tertullian, an early Christian leader from Carthage in the Roman province of Africa, says "*Christ unbelted every soldier.*" Notice the "*all* who draw the sword will die by the sword." Jesus is speaking of Peter who drew his sword in defense of his Lord. The "*all*" makes this *a general principle*. Tertullian wrote: "*Can it be lawful to handle the sword, when the Lord himself has declared that he who uses the sword*

---

25. "Answers to objections to Christian Pacifism."

*shall perish by it?"* The testimony of *the early church is strongly against the use of violence.*[26]

> In Luke, Jesus is recorded as giving an additional rebuke: But Jesus said, *"No more of this!"* And he touched his ear and healed him (Luke 22.51). This might just be to Peter for the situation in the garden. But it might be for all of us who seek to obey Jesus—*no more of this violent self-defense or violent defense of those close and dear to us.*[27]

There is no doubt Jesus was zealous and sympathized with many Zealot views. However, there is also no doubt that while Jesus had a Zealot-like rigorous analysis of the political economy he opposed, he had a very un-Zealot-like generous attitude towards his opponents. He cared for all people, not only Zealots, like Simon, but also tax collectors, like Matthew, whom most Zealots would have seen as a traitor and would have not hesitated to kill. He not only preached "love of enemy," he also practiced "love of enemy," reaching out to the servant of the high priest, who had been struck by a disciple when he had come to arrest Jesus, tenderly healing his ear that had been cut off.

- He criticized the authorities for their corruption and oppression (Mark 10:42; Luke 13:32).
- He wanted to overthrow the status quo by creating a new society in the heart of the old (Luke 6:19–22).
- He sought to establish an upside-down system which would put the first last and the last first (Mark 9:35).
- He drove the rip-off merchants out of the temple, using a whip on the animals, but *not* on the people (John 2:15).
- He said that he came not to bring peace but a call to change which cut through other duties and obligations like a sword (Matt 10:34).
- And he asked his disciples to put their swords back in their place, "for," he said, "all who draw the sword will die by the sword" (Luke 22:36–38).

*Jesus was not a re-active violent revolutionary but a pro-active nonviolent revolutionary—an extraordinary prophetic, compassionate, activist who*

26. Ibid.
27. Ibid.

*embodied the original jihad of nonviolent struggle for inspirational personal growth and transformational social change.*

As Ahmad Shawqi says: "kindness, chivalry, and humility were born the day Jesus was born. Like the light of the dawn flowing through the universe, so did the sign of Jesus flow. He filled the world with light, making the earth shine with its brightness. No threat, no tyranny, no revenge, no sword, no raids, no bloodshed did he use to call to the new faith."[28]

## Nonviolent Sacrificial Compassion

Jesus of Nazareth, whom we know as Jesus the *Masih* (Messiah/Christ), demonstrates a life of radical non-violent sacrificial compassion as the only way of life that can save us from destroying ourselves and our societies.

Many Christians, Muslims, and Jews use the retaliation advocated in the Hebrew Bible to justify their eye-for-an-eye reactive violence. After all Moses himself said, "if there is serious injury, you are to take life for life, eye for eye, tooth for tooth" (Exod 21:23–24). But as Mahatma Gandhi has been often reported to have famously said: "An eye-for-eye and tooth-for-tooth would lead to a world of the blind and toothless."

Thus, Jesus argued for a totally different approach to that taken in the Mosaic law. Jesus explicitly, specifically, and repeatedly contradicted the Mosaic law that legitimated retaliation. He said: "You have heard that it was said, 'Eye for eye, and tooth for tooth.' But I tell you, Do not resist [or retaliate against] an evil person. If someone strikes you on the right cheek, turn to him the other also" (Matt 5:38–39). Jesus told his disciples *you should always be ready to die for your faith, but never kill for your faith* (author's interpretation of Matt 16:24).

Jesus treated the Hebrew Bible, what Christians call the "Old Testament," as his authority (Matt 5:17–20). But he interpreted the Law according to the Prophets, especially Isaiah, whom he quoted at the start of his ministry (Luke 4). Jesus' devotion to peacemaking was inspired by Isaiah's vision for peace. Jesus knew by heart "how beautiful on the mountains are the feet of those who bring good news, who proclaim peace" (Isa 52:7). He knew a bringer of good news would be strong-but-gentle, he "will not shout or cry out, or raise his voice in the streets—a bruised reed he will not break and a smoldering wick he will not quench" (Isa 42:2). The hope he had for

28. Shawqi, *Al-Shawquiyyat*, 12.

his people was that: "no longer w[ould] violence be heard in your land, nor ruin or destruction within your borders" (Isa 60:18).

When I asked my dear friend, Jewish Rabbi, Zalman Kastel, what he personally found most confronting in the teaching of Jesus, he quickly replied, without any hesitation, that it was his commitment to unflinching nonviolence in the face of violence, which was based on his commitment to love everyone—friend and foe alike—with no exceptions.

Jesus said

> But to you who are listening I say, Love your enemies, do good to those who hate you, bless those who curse you, pray for those who ill-use you. To him who strikes you on one cheek offer the other cheek also. If anyone takes away your cloak, do not stop him taking your tunic, too. Give to everyone who asks you; if anyone takes away your belongings, do not demand them back again. As you would like men to act towards you, so do you act towards them. If you love those who love you, what special grace is there in that? Even sinners love those who love them. If you are kind to those who are kind to you, what special grace is there in that? Even sinners love those who love them. If you lend to those from whom you wish to get, what special grace is in that? Even sinners lend to sinners in order to get as much back again. But you must love your enemies; and do good to them; and lend with no hope of getting anything in return. Your reward will be great and you will be the sons of the Most High, because he is kind both to the thankless and to the wicked. Be merciful as your Father in heaven is merciful. (Luke 6:27–38)

The famous Scottish theologian, William Barclay, wrote:

> There is no commandment of Jesus which has caused so much discussion and debate as the commandment to love our enemies. Before we can obey it we must discover what it means. In Greek there are three words for to love. There is *eran,* which describes passionate love, the love of a man for a maid. There is *philein,* which describes our love for our nearest and dearest, the warm affection of the heart. Neither of these two words is used here; the word used here is *agapan,* which needs a whole paragraph to translate it.
>
> *Agapan* describes an active feeling of benevolence towards the other person; it means that no matter what that person does to us we will never allow ourselves to desire anything but his [or her] highest good; and we will deliberately and of set purpose go

out of our way to be good and kind to him [or her]. This is most suggestive. We cannot love our enemies as we love our nearest and dearest. To do so would be unnatural, impossible and even wrong. But we can see to it that, no matter what a [person] does to us, even if he [or she] insults, ill-treats and injures us, we will seek nothing but his [or her] highest good.

This passage has in it two great facts about the ethos of Jesus. Firstly, the ethos of Jesus is positive. It does not consist in *not doing things* but in *doing* them. Jesus gave us the Golden Rule which bids us do to others as we would have them do to us. That rule exists in many writers of many creeds in its negative form. Hillel, one of the great Jewish Rabbis, was asked by a man to teach him the whole law while he stood on one leg. He answered, "What is hateful to thee, do not to another. That is the whole law and all else is explanation." Philo, the great Jew of Alexandria, said, "What you hate to suffer, do not do to anyone else." Socrates, the Greek orator, said, "What things make you angry when you suffer them at the hands of others, do not you do to other people." Every one of these forms is negative. It is not unduly difficult to keep yourself from such action; but it is a very different thing to go out of your way to do to others what you would want them to do to you. The very essence of the ethics of Jesus is that it consists, not in refraining from bad things, but in actively doing good things.

Secondly, the ethos of Jesus is based on *[doing] the extra thing.* Jesus described the common ways of sensible conduct and then dismissed them with the question, "What special grace is in that?" So often people claim to be just as good as their neighbors. Very likely they are. But the question of Jesus is, "How much better are you than the ordinary person?" It is not our neighbor with whom we must compare ourselves; we may well stand that comparison very adequately; it is God with whom we must compare ourselves; and in that comparison we are all in default.

What is the reason for this ethos? As far as Jesus was concerned the reason is it makes us like God, for that is the way he acts. God sends his rain on the just and the unjust. He is kind to the person who brings him joy and equally kind to the person who grieves his heart. God's love embraces saint and sinner alike. It is that love we must copy; if we, too, seek even our enemy's highest good we will in truth be the children of God.[29]

29. Barclay, *Daily Study Bible—Luke 6.* Online: http://www.studylight.org/commentaries/dsb/view.cgi?bk=41&ch=6

John the Baptist introduced Jesus at the beginning of his ministry as the *"Lamb of God* who takes away the sin of the world" (John 1:29). We know the word *"Lamb"* is not meant to be taken literally. After all Jesus was a man not a lamb. However, the word "Lamb" is used to describe the kind of man he was. He was a *"Lamb"* of a man—*pure, simple, and peaceable—not deceitful, duplicitous, and dangerous, like a wolf in sheep's clothing.*

Jesus, the *Lamb of God,* sought to develop grassroots communities of *flocks of sheep* (John 10:11–16). "Sheep" was a seemingly innocuous, but essentially counter-cultural term, that Jesus used to describe *people who lived with "wolves"* (that preyed on other people) *but who refused to become wolves themselves,* even if it meant that the wolves might rip the flock to pieces because of their refusal to join the pack and prey on others.

Jesus said: "I want you to live your lives as sheep, *even in the midst of wolves."* Again, "Be shrewd. *But always be harmless"* (Matt 10:16). *"Always treat other people as you would like them to treat you"* (Matt 7:12). *"Even do good to those who do evil to you. Love those who hate you and bless those who curse you"* (Matt. 5:44). *"Don't ever be afraid"* he said to his flocks, *"of those who can kill the body, but can't kill your soul"* (Matt 10:28).

And Jesus, *the Lamb of God,* practiced what he preached. He may have been "the light of the world." But the world didn't want him. "The people loved the darkness rather than the light; because their deeds were evil, and didn't want anybody to expose them."[30] So the people decided to *scapegoat* him. And, as Jesus predicted, they eventually seized him, and he allowed them to lead him away like a *sacrificial lamb* and slaughter him.[31]

Jesus said: *"Greater love has no one than this, that he lay down his life for his friends"* (John 15:13). The idea of someone being willing to *sacrifice* himself on behalf of his friends can be as powerful a metaphor in the twenty-first century as it was in the first century. There is much about the way the Jews might understand this metaphor that non-Jews find difficult to understand. But the idea that Jesus was willing to *sacrifice* his life for his friends is a powerful story, which even now touches people with love, in the deep, dark, hidden recesses of their soul, where they feel most abandoned and most alone.

Gale Webbe, in *The Night and Nothing* said, "There are many ways to deal with evil. All of them are facets of the truth that *the only ultimate way to conquer evil is to let it be smothered within a willing, living, human being.*

30. John 3:19–20
31. Matt 20:17–19

*When it is absorbed there, like a spear into one's heart, it loses its power and goes no further.*"[32] As Scott Peck says in *The People of the Lie*, "*The healing of evil can only be accomplished by love. A willing sacrifice is required. The healer must sacrificially absorb the evil.*"[33] On the cross Jesus absorbed the evil. He took into his heart as assuredly as the spear that was thrust into his side. And, it went no further. He cried out, "Father, forgive them, for they know not what they do" (Luke 23:24). There was no reaction. No demand for revenge or retaliation. There was only grace. And so the cycle of violence stopped right there and then, with him, forever.

According to Khalid Muhammad Khalid, Jesus was the supreme example. He said Jesus "*was his message. He was the supreme example he left. He was the love which knows no hatred, the peace which knows no restlessness, the salvation which knows no perishing.*"[34]

Mahatma Gandhi said "The gentle figure of Christ—so patient, so kind, so loving, so full of forgiveness that he taught his followers not to retaliate when struck, but to turn the other cheek—was a beautiful example of the perfect person."[35] Jesus, the "martyr, was an embodiment of sacrifice," and the cross "a great example of suffering. . . . Jesus lost his life on the cross. But Jesus didn't lose the battle. Jesus won. As the world's history has abundantly shown. And, consequently, the example of Christ is a crucial factor in the composition of my underlying faith in nonviolence—which rules all my actions."[36]

## A Struggle for Love and Justice

Hans Küng, who is so well regarded for his work in interfaith dialogue at the Parliament of World Religions, is well placed to assess the role Jesus played. Küng says if we put Jesus in the cross co-ordinates of the other options in his own tradition or in other religions, and we compare Jesus in the light of the other options that are presented, then we can see that Jesus plays the role of *a prophetic, compassionate, sacrificial activist in the nonviolent struggle for love and justice*, like no one else we have ever seen in history.

---

32. Webbe, *The Night and Nothing*, 109.
33. Peck, *People of the Lie*, 269.
34. Khalid, *Ma'an 'ala-l-Tariq*, 188–89.
35. Gandhi, *The Message of Jesus*, foreword.
36. Ibid., 7.

Jesus did not try to play the role of a reformist priest, because he was against the establishment. He did not try to play the part of a traditional preacher, because he was against legalism. He did not try to play the part of a classical monk, because he was no ascetic! And he did not take up arms and fight as a guerrilla, because he was against violence—from the left as well as the right.[37]

For Jesus, liberation could never come from Pharisaic rules and regulations, Sadducean rituals and ceremonies, Qumranic disciplines and practices, or Zealot strategies and tactics. For Jesus, liberation could only ever come through love—real love—substantive, sacrificial, giving and forgiving love—love of our God and God's love of our neighbor—love of our friends and love of our enemies.

Jesus did not play the role of a mystic like Buddha, a scholar like Confucius, a lawgiver like Moses, or a military leader like Muhammad. He didn't try to renounce the world and/or study it on the one hand, or try to organize the world and/or control it on the other hand.[38] Jesus loved the world and simply showed people the way that they could love their world like he did.

It was never Jesus' intention to start a religion—still less a monopolistic religion that saw itself in competition with other religions for people's allegiance. Jesus said he simply came "to bring life and life in all its fullness" (see John 10:10). Thus, he would affirm all that is life-affirming and confront all that is life-negating in the world's religions—especially in the religion that now bears his name.

Jesus was critical of domineering leadership in religion—whether in Roman religion or in his own Jewish religion (Mark 10:42–43); acting as closed groups that are not open to others (Matt 5:47); and practicing empty rituals which embody no practical compassion (Matt 6:7).

Jesus appreciated God was bigger than his religion, and worked in the lives of people of other religions—like Naaman the Syrian, who was healed of leprosy, when many Jews weren't (Luke 4:16–30). Jesus appreciated that people of other religions could not only have great faith, but also have greater faith than many people of his own religion—like the Syrophoenician woman, whose feisty faith he was confronted with (Mark 7:24–30). And Jesus appreciated people of other religions could be better examples

---

37. Küng, *Christianity*, 34.

38. Ibid., 35.

of true religion than even the leaders of his own religion—like the Good Samaritan (Luke 10:29–37).

The way Jesus related as a Jew to a Samaritan woman at the well (John 4:4–42) is the way people of different religions, like Christians and Muslims, should relate to each other:

A. Recognize how much we owe to Jews who came before us (John 4:22)

B. Acknowledge particularities—distinct rituals of worship (John 4;19–21)

C. Affirm universalities—all true believers worship in truth (John 4:23)

D. Never denigrate others—don't "call down fire" on them (Luke 9:54–55)

E. Take a conciliatory approach—"if not against you, for you" (Luke 9:50)

F. Always accept hospitality—share food and drink together (John 4:7)

G. Practice respectful dialogue—explore the significance of *Isa*/Jesus as the *Masih*/Messiah—but not expect others to change religion (John 4)

Jesus didn't call his followers to convert others, simply to witness to others. Jesus said "you will receive power when the Holy Spirit comes on you; and you will be my witnesses in Jerusalem, and in all Judea and Samaria, and to the ends of the earth" (Acts 1:8). And he suggested that the best way for anyone to witness was by working whole-heartedly for the common good. Jesus said: "let your light shine before others, that they may see your good works and praise your Father in heaven" (Matt 5:16).

From the moment he was conceived, his mother Mary knew Jesus would be a revolutionary figure: a king who would not only overthrow other kings, but also the very idea of "kingship" itself; an extraordinary man who would stand, with gentle dignity—against relentless cruelty—for the sake of equality. As far as Mary was concerned, Jesus was the answer to her people's prayers (Luke 1:46–55).

Mary is said to have sung a song of praise that reflected her deep, profound, personal faith in God and revealed her joyous and jubilant appreciation of His great faithfulness to her as a person. She sang:

> My soul praises the Lord and my spirit rejoices in God, my Saviour, for He has been mindful of the humble state of His servant. From now on all generations will call me blessed, for the Mighty One has done great things for me—holy is His Name. His mercy

extends to those who fear Him, from generation to generation. (Luke 1:46–50)

Mary's Song has been described by Stanley Jones as "the most revolutionary document in the world."[39] Mary celebrated her experience of God as a God of love and justice, whom she prays will one day have overthrown the rich and the powerful and upheld the poor and the powerless. She sang:

> He has performed mighty deeds with His arm; He has scattered those who are proud in the plans of their hearts. He has brought down the mighty from their thrones, but has lifted up the humble. He has filled the hungry with good things, but has sent the rich away empty. He has helped His servant Israel, remembering to be merciful to Abraham and his descendants forever, even as He said to our fathers. (Luke 1:51–56)

The political economy in which Jesus grew up was one of complete captivity. Palestine was under the complete control of the Roman Empire, abetted by prominent Jewish collaborators. The authorities levied taxes on the population that amounted to 40 percent of people's income. And their taxes were used to maintain the very army of occupation that the people despised. When revolts broke out from time to time, as the people tried to break free of the forces that controlled their lives, the Jewish collaborators aided the Roman colonialists in putting down the rebellions. They cooperated with the very powers that oppressed their own people in order to maintain their position, their property, and their monopoly of the market. Not surprisingly, trade and commerce thrived under *Pax Romana*. And the Great Jewish Temple in Jerusalem, combining the roles of Stock Exchange, Central Bank, and Government Treasury, became the symbol of that prosperity. However, Israel was still essentially an agrarian society, and agriculture was not only the primary industry, but also the premier industry in society. Thus, ownership of land was the main source of wealth. Most of the land was owned by a few rich families, who continued to acquire more and more land as the poor families, who couldn't afford to pay their taxes, were forced to sell more and more of their land to pay the taxes that were imposed on them. The poor people, who found themselves without any land at all, were facing a very bleak future indeed. They were forced to confront a cycle of poverty that entailed not only terrible financial insecurity but also total fiscal vulnerability to the very system which dispossessed

39. Barclay, *The Gospel of Luke*, 9.

them in the first place. In this system the poor, the prisoners, the disabled, the disadvantaged, the lepers, and other marginalized and disadvantaged people, literally had no place to which they could turn for help. They were helpless.[40]

On one balmy Sabbath, at the very beginning of his ministry, Jesus visited the synagogue in his home town of Nazareth, and when he was asked to read a passage from Holy Scripture, he turned to a part, written by the prophet Isaiah, where it says:

> The Spirit of God has got hold of me, and is urging me to take on a special task; to share good news with the poor, to free the prisoners, to help the disabled and the disadvantaged, and to smash the shackles of the oppressed . . . .
> (see Luke 4:18)

In so doing, Jesus announced, in front of everyone he knew at the time, that he wanted to make this radical struggle for God's love and justice his manifesto, his mission in life.

*Jesus grew up with a passionate concern for the welfare of his people, particularly those that no one else was particularly concerned for.* He was passionately concerned about the plight of the poor, the victims of the imperial system. He was passionately concerned about the predicament of the prisoners, the disabled and disadvantaged, excluded from all meaningful participation in society by bars of steel and stigma. He was passionately concerned about the condition of the lepers, not only because of the pain of their ulcers, but also because of the pain of their untouchability. And he was passionately concerned about the situation of ordinary people whose hope had all but been crushed by their soul-destroying circumstances, and who consequently felt consigned forever to long days, and even longer nights, of utter despair.

For Jesus, a passionate concern *for* people meant nothing less than a passionate commitment *to* people. He became forgetful of himself, living instead in constant remembrance of those around him who were themselves forgotten. He desperately wanted them to feel fully alive again, to revel in the joy of being loved, and being able to love, once more. He worked tirelessly to set them free from all that might debilitate them, breaking the bonds of exclusivity, poverty, misery, and guilt. He welcomed the outcast, helped the weak, healed the sick, and forgave the sinner, giving them all

---

40. Andrews, *Christi-Anarchy*, 108–13.

another chance at a new beginning. He didn't write anyone off himself, and he encouraged everyone that he met not to write one another off either. He challenged everyone to tear up their prejudices, trash their stereotypes, and just get their act together—the "in" crowd with the outcast; the strong with the weak; the rich with the poor; the saint with the sinner—to support one another in their common quest for their own humanity.

*Jesus was painfully aware of the captivity of the political economy in which he lived.* He recognized that this captivity was perpetuated by pre-occupation with power, position, and property, at the expense of people's lives. "What the world esteems," Jesus said, "is disgusting to God!" (Luke 16:15). His critique was *universal*, but Jesus actually chose to confront this captivity at a *national* level, rather than an *international* level. Jesus was concerned more with the mechanisms of control perpetuated by his own people, than with the mechanisms of control perpetuated by others, for unless these domestic mechanisms of control were dealt with, the foreign yoke might be thrown off, but the captivity would continue. So Jesus confronted the people in his own country—the people of his own culture, tradition, and religion—with their responsibility for their own captivity, and for their own liberation. "Don't judge others," Jesus said. "Judge yourself" (see Matt 7:1–3). "How sad it is," he said to them, that "you neglect to do justice" (see Luke 11:42). "What will it profit them if they gain the whole world but forfeit their life?" (Matt 16:26).

*In the first phase of his nonviolent jihad for love and justice, Jesus followed on from John the Baptist in denouncing the exploitation of the poor by the rich.* John told the armed forces: "Don't extort money and don't accuse people falsely—be content with your pay." And he told the tax collectors: "Don't collect any more than you are required to." He said, "The man with two tunics should share with him who has none, and the one who has food should do the same" (Luke 3:11–14). Jesus confronted Zacchaeus, an infamous tax collector, personally about his extortion. As a result of this encounter, Zacchaeus promised Jesus to give "half of my possessions to the poor," and "if I have cheated anybody out of anything, I will pay back four times the amount" (Luke 19:8).

*In the second phase of his nonviolent jihad for love and justice Jesus not only consistently denounced the oppression of the powerless by the powerful, he also actively advocated liberation of disempowered groups of people through the empowerment of the Spirit.* Jesus attacked the key religious leaders of the day, as "lovers of money" (Luke 16:14–15), who would maintain a façade of sanctity by saying long prayers in public, but would "devour widows' houses." When he saw a widow "put everything—all she had to live on"—into the collection box, Jesus condemned the temple for extorting the last coin from the kind of person it was set up to protect (Mark 12:38–44). Jesus broke the monopoly on forgiveness that the temple had developed through the sacrificial system it controlled. He did this by baptizing people in the Spirit and giving them the authority to forgive sins. "Receive the Holy Spirit," and "if you forgive anyone his sins, they are forgiven" (John 20:22–23).

*In the third phase of his nonviolent jihad for love and justice Jesus advocated communities with leadership that would serve the people rather than oppress them.* In his countercultural communities, Jesus encouraged people to liberate themselves from captivity to the political economy, by developing compassion for people that transcended the sick, obsessive, compulsive, preoccupation with power, position, and property that characterized society. "God is compassionate," Jesus said. "Be as compassionate as God" (Luke 6:35–36). *All oppressive forms of politics were denounced.* Charismatic leadership, based on experience, was expected to be exercised within a decision-making framework that functioned according to group consensus. "We all know the bosses call the shots, and the heavies throw their weight around," said Jesus. "But that is not the way we are going to operate. Whoever wants to be the leader of a group, should be the servant of the group" (Matt 20:25–26). *All exploitative forms of economics were renounced.* Generosity was expected to be exercised, and wealth freely shared by the rich with the poor, in an earnest quest for genuine equality. "Be on your guard against all kinds of greed," Jesus said (Luke 12:15); "Give to everyone who begs from you, and do not refuse anyone who wants to borrow from you" (Matt. 5:42); "Lend, expecting nothing in return" (Luke 6:35).

*In the fourth phase of his nonviolent jihad for love and justice Jesus created communities that were committed to doing justice to the marginalized and disadvantaged.* The dominant value of much of Jewish society at the time was purity—but the dominant value of Jesus was inclusivity. While many Jews despised Gentiles, Jesus declared "my house shall be called a house ... for all nations" (Mark 11:17). While the Pharisees ostracized sinners, Jesus invited outcasts to his parties (Mark 2:16). In his countercultural communities, Jesus encouraged people to consider other people to be of enormous importance—not just as producers or consumers, but as people in their own right. The people that were usually considered least important, and consequently pushed to the side, were treated as most important and given a place of respect in these countercultural communities. Jesus said: "When you give a luncheon or dinner, do not invite your friends, your brothers, sisters, or relatives, or your rich neighbors; if you do, they may invite you back and you will be repaid. But when you give a banquet, invite the poor, the crippled, the lame, the blind, and you will be blessed. Although they cannot repay you, you will be repaid at the resurrection of the righteous" (Luke 14:12–14).

The counter-cultural communities Jesus developed never smashed the political economy to which their society was captive. They never completely reconstructed the political economy in terms of the total liberation that they prayed for. *However, they did break some of the mechanisms of control to which they were captive. They managed to reconstruct such a substantial degree of liberated—and liberating—alternative political and economic reality, that their experience has served as an example of true love and true justice ever since.* According to eyewitnesses, they all met together, breaking bread in their homes and eating together with glad and jubilant hearts. They had everything in common, selling their possessions and giving support to anyone who asked for help. There wasn't a single person with an unmet need among them, and all the people spoke well of them (see Acts 2:44–47; 4:32–35).

*In the fifth phase of his nonviolent jihad for love and justice Jesus demonstrated active, radical, sacrificial nonviolence that would free people from the cycles of violence and counter violence.* He said:

> I am the good shepherd. The good shepherd lays down his life for the sheep. The hired hand is not the shepherd who owns the sheep. So when he sees the wolf coming, he abandons the sheep and runs away. Then the wolf attacks the flock and scatters it. The man runs away because he is a hired hand and cares nothing for the sheep. I am the good shepherd . . . and I lay down my life for the sheep. All who ever came before me were thieves and robbers. I am the gate; whoever enters through me will be saved. He will come in and go out, and find pasture. The thief comes only to steal and destroy; I have come that they may have life, and have it to the full. (John 10:8–18)

Jesus turned to his friends and said: "Greater love has no one than this, that he lay down his life for his friends" (John 15:13).

Under his guidance the Jesus movement became an active, radical, sacrificial peace movement.[41] And for three centuries, Christianity was more or less a pacifist movement. The apostles taught Christians the pacifist principle: "Love does no harm to its neighbor" (Rom 13:10); Paul said,

> Bless those who persecute you; bless and do not curse. Do not repay anyone evil for evil. Be careful to do what is right in the eyes of everybody. If it is possible, as far as it depends on you, live at peace with everyone. Do not take revenge. On the contrary: "If your enem[ies] are hungry, feed [them]; if [they] are thirsty, give [them] something to drink." Do not be overcome by evil, but overcome evil with good.
> (Rom 12:14–21)

It seems that *the testimony of the early church was against violence of any sort.* Hippolytus, the most important third-century theologian in the Christian Church in Rome, wrote in *The Apostolic Tradition*, about 218 C.E., *"A civic magistrate who wears the purple and governs by the sword shall give it up. If a military constable is commanded to kill in the course of his duty, he must not take this upon himself."*[42] While Athenagoras, a second-century Greek philosopher, who converted to Christianity, wrote in *A Plea Regarding Christians*, "[We] are not even allowed to hit back when struck and are expected to use only kind words when reviled! To be just alone is not enough because to be just means to repay like for like, but we have been commanded to go far beyond this, to be kind and patient."[43]

Jesus was a supreme example of *Jihad* as a "strong-but-gentle struggle."

41. Stassen and Gushee, *Kingdom Ethics*, 152.

42. "Answers to Objections to Christian Pacifism." Online: http://www.plowcreek.org/answers.htm

43. Ibid.

Consider the approach Jesus took to his nonviolent *jihad* for love and justice

1. *In the first phase of his nonviolent jihad for love and justice Jesus followed on from John the Baptist in denouncing the exploitation of the poor by the rich.*

2. *In the second phase of his nonviolent jihad for love and justice Jesus denounced the oppression of the powerless by the powerful and actively advocated liberation of disempowered groups of people through the power of the Spirit.*

3. *In the third phase of his nonviolent jihad for love and justice Jesus advocated communities with leadership that would serve rather than oppress people.*

4. *In the fourth phase of his nonviolent jihad for love and justice Jesus created communities committed to doing justice to the marginalized & disadvantaged.*

5. *In the fifth phase of his nonviolent jihad for love and justice Jesus demonstrated active, radical, sacrificial nonviolence to free people from the cycles of violence.*

# 6

## Recollecting Strong-But-Gentle Nonviolent Struggles

If we are to engage in "strong-but-gentle nonviolent struggles" we need to recollect true stories that can inspire us to act and that, as case studies, can instruct us how we can act.

Let me share with you four true stories—two from the past and two from the present—that can serve as case studies in radical, practical, Christian/Muslim nonviolent struggle.

The first recollection is of a Christian, Francesco Bernadone, better known as Francis of Assisi, also known as the "Juggler." The second recollection is of a Muslim, Khan Abdul Ghaffar Khan, better known as Badshah Khan, also as the "Khan." The third recollection is of another Christian, Leymah Gbowee, also known as the "General." The fourth recollection is of another Muslim, Muhammad Ashafa, better known as the "Imam."

### Francis of Assisi—
### "Lord Make Me an Instrument of Thy Peace"

Francis was born to a French mother and Italian father in 1182, and his father called him Francesco—or Francis—after a trip to France. The "little Frenchman" was brought up on romantic French ballads sung by traveling troubadours. The son of a wealthy merchant, Francis led a cavalier life in his youth, and was considered the life of the party by his contemporaries.

Francis grew up with the dream that one day he would become a knight. So, in his early twenties, Francis took to the opportunity to fight for Assisi against a neighboring town. However, his haughty military career came to an abrupt halt when the young Francis was captured and incarcerated.

This time was to prove a turning point for Francis. For, during the year in prison and the year in convalescence following his release, Francis thought long and hard about his life. His dream of becoming a knight seemed ridiculous in the light of the harsh reality of war that had confronted him.

One day, when Francis was riding along a road, he simply stopped dead in his tracks. It was as if he could not carry on any more as he was. He dismounted, undressed, then—bit by bit—took all his knightly regalia—including his horse, and his sword and his armor—and gave it all away.

His father became exasperated with Francis over his prodigality with the family's property and so he organized a meeting with the local bishop to pull him into line. But it backfired big time. Francis responded to his father's complaints by renouncing his family, and his family's property, altogether.

Right there and then he gave back everything his family had given him. Including the clothes that he was wearing at the time. So that Francis stood there naked as the day that he was born. Then he turned to his father and said: "Until now I have called you father, but from now on I can say without reserve, 'Our Father who is in Heaven'—He is all my wealth—I place my confidence in Him."

In order to consider his future, Francis decided to spend some time living as a hermit beside an old church in San Damiano. While there Francis heard a voice calling him, saying, "Rebuild my church." Francis responded to the call by repairing the ruins of the church in San Damiano, then set about the task of reforming the life of the church throughout Italy.

Francis approached the task of renewal not as a legislator, but as a juggler! He had been brought up with troubadours coming to his house, singing romantic ballads that stirred the heart; and he aspired to be like one of the jugglers who accompanied the troubadours, drawing the crowds for the musicians, so they could listen to the music of the heart that they played. As *Le Jongleur de Dieu*, a "Juggler for God," Francis wanted to travel from town to town, like an entertainer, without a penny to his name, introducing people to *joie de vivre*, the "true joy of living."

Considering his views, it is quite remarkable that Francis did not rage against the pompous opulence of the rich in medieval society. Instead, ever the romantic, Francis tried to woo the people away from their preoccupation with the trappings of power, and get them to fall in love with the lovely "Lady Poverty." Poverty was not an end in itself. But, as far as Francis was concerned, people needed to be willing to be able to joyfully embrace poverty in order to follow the way of Jesus and joyfully embrace the poor.

In 1210 Francis obtained approval for a simple rule dedicated to apostolic poverty. He called the order the Friars Minor, and this band of "little brothers" followed the example of their founder in caring for the poor.

Then in 1212 Clare—a wealthy friend from Assisi; who, like Francis, had been converted, and had given all her wealth to the poor—started a sister order to the brothers, that was to become known as the Poor Clares.

Francis and Clare set about their task with such enthusiasm that people all over the place wanted to join them. And, as hundreds and thousands of people joined in from all over Europe, the humble movement began to gradually engage and eventually change the Dark Age in which they lived.

Francis and Clare undermined feudalism simply by encouraging all their brothers and sisters to lay aside their weapons, unlock the gates, welcome outsiders in, and gladly share their wealth with the poor.

At this time many Christians understood "mission" in terms of the Crusades—which involved the slaughter of many Muslims "in the name of the Lord." Francis not only refused to take up weapons himself, he actually traveled to Egypt where the crusaders were fighting, walking up and down the lines, begging them to lay down their swords.

When they would not listen to him, Francis crossed the lines at Damietta, and went to talk with the "enemy" sultan, Mele-el-Khamil, to tell him about the "Prince of Peace," and to try to broker a peace deal "in his name."

While Francis was overseas disputes arose among the Friars. A Vicar-General was appointed to take control of the order, and a revised set of organizational rules were instituted, which were to change the character of the movement quite considerably.

Holding on to his original calling Francis withdrew from leadership and retired to a hermitage on Monte Alvernia where the man we know as St. Francis died in 1226.

The political philosopher, John Ralston Saul, says "Francis of Assisi [and his followers] were the most famous activists [of their day]. To a great extent they laid out the modern democratic model of inclusion—an important step towards egalitarianism. [They] took the elements of personal responsibility, set out tantalizingly in the New Testament, and imagined a social model which . . . would change our societies."[1]

1. Saul, *The Unconscious Civilization*, 136–37.

All of us who would engage in strong-but-gentle struggle for justice against injustice would do well to pray the prayer of St. Francis:

> Lord make me an instrument of thy peace.
> Where there is hatred, let me sow love;
> Where there is injury, pardon;
> Where there is doubt, faith;
> Where there is despair, hope;
> Where there is darkness, light;
> Where there is sadness, joy.
>
> O Divine Master,
> Grant that I
> may not so much seek
> To be consoled, as to console;
> Not so much to be understood, as to understand;
> Not so much to be loved, as to love;
> For it is in giving that we receive;
> It is in pardoning that we are pardoned;
> And it is in dying that we are raised to eternal life.

## Consider the inner dynamics of this *jihad:*

1. *Trust in God*—my confidence is in Him.
2. *Rejoice in God*—the true joy of living.
3. *Do God's will*—make me an instrument.
4. *Be like Jesus*—follow the way of Jesus.
5. *Reject status*—no trappings of power.
6. *Renounce riches*—he gave it all away.
7. *Embrace the poor*—embrace the poor.
8. *Stay proactive*—where there is hatred sow love.

## Consider the outer dynamics of this *jihad:*

1. *Raise consciousness*—where there is despair, bring hope.
2. *Encourage commitment*—where there is doubt, bring faith.
3. *Organize groups*—bands of brothers/sisters.
4. *Implement discipline*—a simple rule of life.
5. *Embody compassion*—to love and to console.
6. *Practice nonviolence*—instruments of peace.
7. *Oppose violence*—refuse to use weapons.
8. *Promote justice*—inclusivity and equity.
9. *Resist crusades*—refuse to fight against "infidels."
10. *Resolve conflicts*—talk with the "enemy."

# Badshah Khan—
# I Promise to Serve Humanity in the Name of God

Abdul Ghaffar Khan was born in Utmanzai in 1890. His father, Behram Khan, was a wealthy Pathan who ran a large guest house on the main road to Peshawar. Behram Khan had many servants, but he always took great pride in serving his honored guests himself. His mother—whose name I do not know—lived her life, like most Pathan women, in *purdah*, hidden from prying eyes behind a veil of secrecy. She was reputedly quite devout, and set her son an unforgettable example of genuine piety.

In 1901 Ghaffar Khan attended Edwards Memorial School in Peshawar. The headmaster, Rev. Wigram, a stern but generous teacher, was committed to providing the best education he could for the boys on the Northwest Frontier. And the young Ghaffar Khan grew to appreciate him almost as much as his own parents. Not surprisingly, in 1910, after spending a couple of years in the Islamic School in Aligarh, Ghaffar Khan started a school in Utmanzai, his own home town.

In 1913 Ghaffar Khan participated in a conference of progressive Muslims that was held in Agra. He met famous Islamic leaders, like Maulana Azad, and he seized the chance to discuss his understanding of Islam with them. "It is my inmost conviction," he was to say later, "that Islam is *amal* (work), *yakeen* (faith), and *muhabat* (love), and without these the name Muslim is sounding brass and tinkling cymbal."[2]

Upon returning to the Northwest Frontier after the conference, Ghaffar Khan decided to perform a *chilla,* or fast, in order to seek divine guidance on how he could put the *amal, yakeen,* and *muhabat* that he preached into practice. What actually occurred during the *chilla* no one knows. But we do know that Ghaffar Khan emerged from the fast with a resolute determination to serve God as fully as he could for the rest of his life.

In 1915, his wife, whom he married in 1912, died of influenza. Ghaffar Khan set out on a pilgrimage to visit every village in the Northwest Frontier. Three years—and five hundred villages—later, Ghaffar Khan returned, saying:

> I have one great desire. I want to rescue these gentle people from the tyranny of the foreigners who have disgraced them. I want to kiss the ground where their ruined homes once stood. I want to wash the stains of blood from their garments. I want to create for them a world of freedom, where they can live in peace, and be happy.[3]

In 1919 Ghaffar Khan was arrested by the British authorities, who saw him as a threat to their power in the region. And, over the next five years, Ghaffar Khan was in and out of prison all the time for nonviolently protesting against British imperialism. On one occasion, he found himself

2. Easwaran, *A Man to Match His Mountains,* 63.

3. Ibid., foreword.

grinding corn in solitary confinement. His fellow prisoners offered to pay a bribe to get him out of prison. But he refused. His prison guard told him he could stop grinding corn if he wanted to. But he replied, "Robbers grind corn. And their cause is impure. Why should I mind grinding, for my cause which is pure?"[4]

In 1924, after a three-year stretch, Ghaffar Khan was released from prison, and he took the opportunity to go on a pilgrimage to Mecca. He was fascinated with the life of the Prophet. Especially the early years, when Mohammed spent his time in Mecca. And he came back from his *hajj* refreshed, ready to re-engage in the struggle for freedom, armed with the "weapon of the Prophet."

"The weapon of the Prophet," he says, "is *sabr*, not *a sabre.*" *Sabr* literally means patience. "The weapon of the Prophet is patience. If you exercise patience, endure all hardships, victory will be yours. No power on earth can stand against it." He quotes the *Qur'an* as saying, "there is no compulsion in religion; forgive and be indulgent; render not vain your almsgiving by injury; whosoever killeth one—for other than manslaughter—it shall be as if he had killed all mankind, and whoso saveth the life of one, it shall be as if he had saved the life of all mankind."[5]

In 1928 Ghaffar Khan started a newspaper called the *Pakhtun*. It was to become the vehicle that he was to use to rally his people for the long ongoing struggle. Then, the following year, Ghaffar Khan launched one of the most exciting, creative, and effective nonviolent campaigns for independence ever conducted. It began innocuously enough with the Khan calling Pathans to join him in forming a movement called the *Khudai Khidmatgar*. Any Pathan could join the movement, provided they swore an oath to become a Servant of God:

> I am a Khudai Khidmatgar, and as God needs no service
>
> I promise to serve humanity in the name of God.
>
> I promise to refrain from violence, and from taking revenge.
>
> I promise to forgive those who oppress me or treat with cruelty.
>
> I promise to refrain from taking part in feuds and quarrels.
>
> I promise to treat every Pathan as my neighbor and friend.
>
> I promise to live a simple life, to practice virtue, and refrain from evil.

4. Ibid., 88–89.

5. Ibid., 117, 209.

I promise to devote at least two hours a day to social work.[6]

It was a brilliant idea—culturally appropriate and politically astute. And Pathans responded to the Khan's call by rallying behind the banner of the Khidmatgar in their thousands. In fact, the recruiting drive was so successful that at one point up to one hundred thousand Pathans—men and women both—donned their famous red shirts, and went to work in the villages, singing:

> We serve and we love; our people and our cause.
> Freedom is our longing; our lives the price we pay.[7]

The courage of these Khudai Khidmatgar was legendary. A British officer commanded a Khidmatgar by the name of Faiz Mohammed to take off his red shirt. He refused. The officer then commanded his soldiers to forcibly strip the recalcitrant. Faiz Mohammed did not fight back, but he refused to cooperate. It took up to nine soldiers to strip him of his proud red shirt. And even then they only were able to do it when they had beaten the Khidmatgar unconscious. The soldiers then came for a Khidmatgar by the name of Mohammed Naquib. He was beaten mercilessly and his shirt was stripped off his back. But when he was ordered to take his trousers off he went berserk. He turned to run to get a gun. But he was pulled up short by the voice of his commander. "Mohammed Naquib!" he cried. "Is your patience is exhausted so soon? You swore to remain nonviolent until death!" With those words ringing in his ears, eyewitnesses say the chastened Khidmatgar turned back to face his tormentors, armed only with the "weapon of the Prophet," fortitude and forbearance.

A large crowd gathered in Kissa Khani Bazaar in Peshawar to protest the brutality of the British. Troops from a nearby army base were deployed. The troops asked the people to disperse; and they had begun to do so, when, without warning, three armored cars drove at speed into the crowd. Several people were run over and were killed on the spot. The troops asked the people to disperse; but they said they would do so only if the armored cars withdrew, and they were allowed to carry away their fallen comrades. The troops did not remove their armored cars, and refused to allow the people remove their fallen comrades. So the crowd did not disperse. The troops then opened fire, shooting point blank range into the front row of

6. Ibid., 110–12.

7. Ibid., 113.

the gathered throng. When those in the front row fell wounded, the next row came forward and took their place. Over and over again, from 11 am in the morning till 5 pm in the evening, row upon row of Khidmatgars, took the place of their fallen comrades, bared their breasts, and were shot to death by the troops. Two to three hundred were killed—many more were wounded—and the bazaar was littered with piles of bodies of the dead and dying. The elite Garhwal Rifles were brought into deal with the crowd. But faced with unarmed men and women, who would not fight, they refused to fire. "We will not shoot our unarmed brethren!" they said. It was the beginning of the end for the empire.[8]

In the aftermath, Ghaffar Khan was arrested. So he spent most of his time—from 1930 to 1945—fighting for independence from prison. After independence, Ghaffar Khan was finally released from prison; but he was rearrested, and thrown into prison once again, this time by the Pakistani government.

Ghaffar Khan had always supported Maulana Azad in his struggle for a liberal, secular, united, democratic country; and that had put him in conflict with Mohamed Ali Jinnah and the Muslim League's agenda for a Muslim State.

Khan said he feared a state founded on a religion—any religion—as he thought it would tend to discriminate against minorities. When Jinnah accused Khan of being less than earnest in his religion, he replied: "I learned [my] secularism from the Koran Sharif." But it was not a view shared by the President of the "Land of the Pure." And as a result the redoubtable dissident was forced to spend most of the rest of his life—from 1948 to 1988—either in jail in Pakistan, or in exile in Afghanistan, where he finally died.

When Nobel Peace Prize Winner, Malala Yousafzai, the courageous young Pakistani education activist, shot by the Taliban, spoke at the United Nations, she made explicit reference to the inspiration of Muhammad, Jesus, Buddha, and others, including Badshah Khan. She said:

> Dear Friends, on the 9th of October 2012, the Taliban shot me on the left side of my forehead. They shot my friends too. They thought that the bullets would silence us. But they failed. And then, out of that silence came, thousands of voices. The terrorists thought that they would change our aims and stop our ambitions but nothing changed in my life except this: Weakness, fear and hopelessness died. Strength, power and courage was born. I am

8. Ibid., 122–24.

the same Malala. My ambitions are the same. My hopes are the same. My dreams are the same.

Dear sisters and brothers, I am not against anyone. Neither am I here to speak in terms of personal revenge against the Taliban or any other terrorists group. I am here to speak up for the right of education of every child. I want education for the sons and the daughters of all the extremists, especially the Taliban.

I do not even hate the Talib who shot me. Even if there is a gun in my hand and he stands in front of me, I would not shoot him. This is the compassion that I have learnt from Muhammad (the prophet of mercy), Jesus Christ. and Lord Buddha. . . . This is the philosophy of nonviolence that I have learnt from (Mahatma) Gandhi, Badshah Khan, and Mother Teresa. And this is the forgiveness that I have learnt from my mother and father.

This is what my soul is telling me, be peaceful and love everyone.

All of us who would engage in strong-but-gentle struggle for justice against injustice would do well to take Badshah Khan's Oath to become "a servant of God":

I am a Khudai Khidmatgar, and as God needs no service . . .

I promise to serve humanity in the name of God.

I promise to refrain from violence, and from taking revenge.

I promise to forgive those who oppress me or treat with cruelty.

I promise to refrain from taking part in feuds and quarrels.

I promise to treat every [person] as my neighbor and friend.

I promise to live a simple life, to practice virtue, and refrain from evil.

I promise to devote at least two hours a day to social work.[9]

9. Ibid., 110–12.

## Consider the inner dynamics of this *jihad*

1. *Act for God*—in the spirit of *Bismillah*.

2. *Advocate Islam*—as true *yakeen* (faith).

3. *Incarnate Islam*—as real *muhabat* (love).

4. *Demonstrate Islam*—as hard *amal* (work).

5. *Give generously*—to all Pathans bar none.

6. *Forgive graciously*—renounce quarrels and cruelty.

7. *Live simply*—suffering the loss of many things.

8. *Serve humanity*—as the one thing that matters.

## Consider the outer dynamics of this *jihad*

1. *Begin movement*—freedom from tyranny.

2. *Recruit participants*—Khudai Khidmatgar.

3. *Secure commitment*—by swearing an oath.

4. *Ensure conduct*—nonviolent warrior code.

5. *Criticize status quo*—with multiple media.

6. *Display alternative*—in community programs.

7. *Oppose injustices*—by public demonstrations.

8. *Accept consequences*—prison, torture, death.

9. *Practice forgiveness*—never ever take revenge.

10. *Embrace patience*—"the weapon of the Prophet."

# Leymah Gbowee—
# We Must Gather the Women and Pray for Peace!

Leymah Gbowee was born in Monrovia, Liberia in 1972. Leymah attended private school, served in the student council, and dreamed of being a doctor. In 1989 The First Liberian Civil War broke out, throwing the country into chaos, and shattering her dreams. Thousands of people were killed and many women were violated. So Leymah fled with her mother and sisters on a boat to Ghana. Leymah says she almost starved to death in the refugee camp, and so, in spite of the risks, she decided to return to Liberia.

"As the war subsided," Leymah Gbowee says, "I learned about a program run by UNICEF training people to be social workers who would then counsel those traumatized by war."[10] This course helped Leymah make a link between the violence she had suffered in her own home in a series of abusive relationships and the violence other women suffered in the war at the hands of both the government and guerilla militias—and out of this sense of solidarity Leymah's struggle for peace and justice was born.

In 1998, Leymah Gbowee enrolled in an Associate of Arts degree and volunteered with the Trauma Healing and Reconciliation Program (THRP), a program operating out of St. Peter's Lutheran Church in Monrovia that she had attended as a teenager and that had been active in peace efforts ever since the civil war started. To begin with Leymah was assigned the task of trying to rehabilitate former child soldiers.

In 1999 The Second Liberian Civil War broke out, throwing the country into chaos and, faced with another "boys war," Leymah Gbowee realized "if any changes were to be made in society it had to be by the mothers."[11]

Her supervisor in the Trauma Healing and Reconciliation Program, whom she calls BB, encouraged Leymah to study peacebuilding, starting with John Howard Yoder's *The Politics of Jesus*, the works of Mahatma Gandhi and Martin Luther King, "and the Ethiopian author and conflict and reconciliation expert Hizkias Assefa."[12] BB also introduced her to the West Africa Network for Peacebuilding (WANEP).[13]

"WANEP was actively seeking to involve women in its work and I was invited to a conference in Ghana," wrote Leymah Gbowee.[14] Through WANEP, Leymah met Thelma Ekiyor of Nigeria, who was "well educated, a lawyer who specialized in alternative dispute resolution."[15] Thelma told

---

10. Gbowee, *Mighty Be Our Powers*, 50.

11. "2009 Gruber Foundation Women's Rights Prize." Gruberprizes.org. Online: http://gruber.yale.edu/womens-rights/press/2009-gruber-womens-rights-prize-press-release

12. Gbowee, *Mighty Be Our Powers*, 88.

13. "WANEP." Online: http://www.wanep.org/wanep/about-us-our-story/about-us.html.

14. Gbowee, *Mighty Be Our Powers*, 101.

15. Ibid., 107–8.

Leymah of her idea to start a women's organization. "Thelma was a thinker, a visionary, like BB. But she was a woman, like me."[16]

Within a year Thelma had managed to get the funding from WANEP to set up the Women in Peacebuilding Network (WIPNET) and Leymah Gbowee had taken on the unpaid position of the WIPNET leader in Liberia.

In 2002, with her five children, "now including an adopted daughter named Lucia Malou, living in Ghana under her sister's care,"[17] Leymah Gbowee was spending her days working on trauma-healing and her evenings working on peace-building. "Falling asleep in the WIPNET office one night, she [had] a dream where she says God had told her, 'Gather the women and pray for peace!'"[18]

Leymah Gbowee believed the voice she heard was from God, but didn't believe it was the job was for her. "She didn't feel worthy. After all, she was living with a man who was married to another woman. 'If God was going to speak to someone in Liberia, it wouldn't be to me!' she thought. Some friends helped her to understand that the task was not meant for others, as she thought; but for her to act upon it herself."[19]

So Leymah Gbowee ran a training session and began organizing a peace prayer campaign. Because the war was being fought between a so-called "Christian" president and a so-called "Muslim" opposition, Leymah, a Christian, intentionally collaborated with Asatu, a Muslim woman. They started "going to the mosques on Friday at noon after prayers, to the markets on Saturday morning, to two churches every Sunday."[20]

Working across religious lines, ("Does the bullet know Christian from Muslim?")[21] the Women of Liberia Mass Action for Peace "started with a few local women praying and singing in a fish market"[22] and eventually became a mass movement of thousands of Christian and Muslim women gathering in Monrovia for months. "They prayed for peace, using Muslim and Christian prayers, and held daily nonviolent demonstrations

16. Ibid., 109.

17. Ibid., 148.

18. Ibid., 122.

19. Hamlin, "Leymah Gbowee and the Hard Work of Faith."

20. Gbowee, *Mighty Be Our Powers*, 126.

21. Ibid., 129.

22. "Peace warrior for Liberia." *Intent blog,* July 20, 2009. Online: http://intentblog.com/leymah-gbowee-peace-warrior-liberia/

and sit-ins in defiance of orders from the tyrannical president at that time, Charles Taylor."[23]

To make themselves more recognizable, "all of the women wore T-shirts that were white, signifying peace, and white hair ties."[24] They handed out flyers, which read: "We are tired! We are tired of our children being killed! We are tired of being raped! Women, wake up—you have a voice in the peace process!" They "also handed out simple drawings explaining their purpose to the many women who couldn't read."[25]

They staged protests, which included the threat of a sex strike—saying that as many of them as they could would refuse to have sex with their partners until they stopped fighting, laid down their weapons and made peace. Leymah Gbowee says, "The [sex] strike lasted, on and off, for a few months. It had little or no practical effect, but it was extremely valuable in getting us media attention [for our campaign]."[26]

On April 23, 2003, Taylor finally granted the women a hearing. "With more than 2,000 women amassed outside his executive mansion," Leymah Gbowee was the person designated to speak for them. She said:

> We are tired of war. We are tired of running. We are tired of begging for bulgur wheat. We are tired of our children being raped. We are now taking this stand, to secure the future of our children. Because we believe, as custodians of society, tomorrow our children will ask us, "Mama, what was your role during the crisis"[27]

Their role that day was to pressure the President into promising to attend peace talks in Ghana to negotiate with the LURD and MODEL rebel groups who were fighting against his government. And they succeeded.

But the peace talks in Ghana dragged on through June and July without any progress, while the killing, looting, and raping continued unabated in Liberia. So Leymah Gbowee led a group of hundreds of Liberian women (many of them refugees in Ghana) to hold a sit-in at the hotel where the talks were being held, holding signs screaming silently: "Butchers and murderers of the Liberian people—STOP!"[28]

23. Gbowee, *Mighty Be Our Powers*, 128, 135.
24. Ibid., 136.
25. Ibid., 127.
26. Ibid., 147.
27. Ibid., 140–41.
28. Ibid., 161.

The women said they would stay sitting in the hallway, holding the delegates "hostage" until a peace agreement was reached. General Abuba-kar (a former president of Nigeria) who proved to be sympathetic to the women, announced with some amusement: "The peace hall has been seized by General Leymah and her troops." When the men tried to leave the hall, Leymah and her allies threatened to rip their clothes off: "In Africa, it's a terrible curse to see a married or elderly woman deliberately bare herself." With Abubakar's support, the women remained sitting outside the negoti-ating room during the following days, ensuring that the "atmosphere at the peace talks changed from circuslike to somber."[29]

The Liberian war ended officially weeks later, with the signing of the Accra Comprehensive Peace Agreement on August 18, 2003.[30] "But what we [women] did marked the beginning of the end."[31] As part of the peace agreement the President, Charles Taylor, was sent into exile. And, as a result of the women's movement, Ellen Johnson Sirleaf was inaugurated as the first elected woman President in Africa.

In 2011 Leymah Gbowee and Ellen Johnson Sirleaf were awarded the Nobel Peace Prize (with Tawakei Karmen) "for their nonviolent struggle for the safety of women and for women's rights to full participation in peace-building work."[32]

Leymah Gbowee "has continued her work in peace and conflict reso-lution, and is now leading the Liberia Reconciliation Initiative, one of the six coordinating organizations that created and guides the roadmap of resolution. She is the President of the Gbowee Peace Foundation Africa, based in Monrovia, and also serves as the Executive Director of Women, Peace and Security Network Africa (WIPSEN-Africa)."[33]

All of us who would engage in strong-but-gentle struggle for justice against injustice would do well to gather a group of friends, watch a DVD of the brilliant documentary *Pray the Devil Back to Hell*, about Leymah Gbowee and the interfaith women's peace movement in Liberia, and dis-cuss what we can learn from their story for our struggle.

29. Ibid., 161–62.

30. Ibid., 164.

31. Ibid., 163.

32. "The Nobel Peace Prize 2011—Press Release." Nobelprize.org. Online: http://www.nobelprize.org/nobel_prizes/peace/laureates/2011/press.html

33. "Leymah Gbowee." In *Nobel Peace Laureates,* Peace Jam. Online: http://www.peacejam.org/laureates/Leymah-Gbowee-13.aspx

## Consider the inner dynamics of this *jihad:*

1. *Listen to God*—God says "you need to act."

2. *Take step one*—to live with the people.

3. *Take step two*—to listen to the people.

4. *Take step three*—to learn from the people.

5. *Take step four*—to analyze the issues raised.

6. *Take step five*—to study nonviolent options.

7. *Take step six*—to explore alternatives to war.

8. *Take step seven*—to prayerfully work for peace.

## Consider the outer dynamics of this *jihad*

1. *Create associations*—for peace-building.

2. *Develop networks*—by building bridges.

3. *Bridge religions*—Christians and Muslims.

4. *Pray together*—for faith to stop a civil war.

5. *Do protests*—sit-ins, sing-ins, sex-strikes.

6. *Defy orders*—to desist, disperse, and be silent.

7. *Confront foes*—both government and guerillas.

8. *Facilitate meetings*—for talks between factions.

9. *Persuade parties*—to agree to a peace settlement.

10. *Monitor outcomes*—exit dictator, enter democracy.

# Muhammad Ashafa—
## A Common God, Shared Values, and Moral Principles

Muhammad Ashafa was born in Mani Katsina State, Northern Nigeria, into a very devout conservative Muslim family, the eldest son of an Islamic scholar and Tijaniyya leader, from a long line of Imams, dating back thirteen generations, who had resisted colonization.

Muhammad Ashafa says that he did not follow in his father's *Sufi* tradition, which was spiritual and anti-materialistic and treated politics as essentially a dirty thing. Instead, like many others of his generation, the young Muhammad was influenced by *Salafi* preachers from Saudi Arabia, the Muslim Brotherhood in Egypt, and the Islamic Revolution in Iran, which led him to join an extremist reformist movement, committed to the total Islamization of northern Nigeria and the complete exclusion of non-Muslims. Muhammad Ashafa became the Secretary General of the Muslim Youth Councils (MYCs) "which incited great violence in the North and resulted in the Christians creating their own counter organization, the Youth Christian Association of Nigeria (YCAN)."[34]

The Secretary General of the Kaduna State chapter of the Youth Christian Association of Nigeria (YCAN) was James Wuye. James was a militant Assemblies of God Pastor, the son of a soldier who served in the Biafran war, who had always been interested in war games, and had got involved in increasingly combative Christian-Muslim encounters. James says his "hatred for the Muslims had no limits." James hated seeing Christians being intimidated by Muslims, so "when Muslims were blamed for inciting a violent conflict in Kaduna, he immediately volunteered to lead a reprisal attack."[35] In the battles that ensued between the rival MYC and YCAN fighters, which Muhammad and James led, Muhammad's mentor and two of his cousins were killed and James lost his right arm.[36]

And Muhammad and James vowed to get revenge, by killing the other, when they could.

About that time, Muhammad was participating in Friday prayers, when an Imam preached a sermon on the *Qur'anic* call not to seek revenge, but instead to extend forgiveness to our enemies. Muhammad felt God was speaking directly to him about forgiving James.[37]

Not long after, a mutual friend, Idriaz Musa, took the opportunity in a chance meeting to get them to together. Idriaz, who was working with Muslim and Christian youth groups against drug addiction, knew both

---

34. "Imam Muhammad Ashafa." Ara Pacis Initiative. Online: http://www.arapacisinitiative.org/en/events-ans-news/35-imam-mohammad-ashafa

35. Ibid.

36. Ibid.

37. Channer, *The Imam and the Pastor Initiative of Change*, FLT Films, 2006.

Muhammad and James, and invited both of them to a meeting about substance abuse. James says

> during the tea or coffee break, he drew us together. He put our hands over each other's hands and said to us, "I know you have the capacity to [make] peace. I want you to talk." And then he just left us there. We were holding hands and looking at each other in a puzzled way. [Muhammad] asked if we could meet. I gave him my office address. He came there, and that begun the journey.[38]

To begin with James Wuye was most suspicious of Muhammad Ashafa. James thought Muhammad was setting him up in order to organize an ambush so he could assassinate him as payback. After all, James says, Muhammad "looked like a fanatic" and fanatics kill without compunction. However Muhammad kindly visited James' mother when she was ill in hospital and quietly came to the funeral to pay his respects when his mother died. And, ever so gently, Muhammad gradually won James' trust, confidence, and friendship.[39]

In 1995, out of their friendship, these two erstwhile enemies, created the Interfaith Mediation Center (IMC) in the State of Kaduna in northern Nigeria. To begin with both the Muslim and Christian communities were suspicious of the IMC. Muhammad says the stereotypes of Christians "run very deep in the heart of many Muslims. There are over one billion of us and many are affected by these stereotypes and [related] suspicions."[40] However, in the same way Muhammad had overcome James' suspicions, "The Imam and The Pastor," as they became known, working together in the light of their declared faith in "a common God, shared values, and moral principles," gradually earned their trust too.[41]

The Interfaith Mediation Center (IMC) leads seminars and workshops in schools and universities on subjects from democracy to interreligious dialogue. Religion "as a factor of rapprochement, is presented as part of their method." The IMC works with religious and political leaders, men and women and youth, training them in conflict resolution.[42]

---

38. "A Discussion with Pastor James Wuye and Imam Muhammad Ashafa." Berkley Center. Online: http://berkleycenter.georgetown.edu/interviews/a-discussion-with-pastor-james-wuye-and-imam-muhammad-ashafa

39. Channer, *The Imam and the Pastor Initiative of Change*.

40. "A Discussion with Pastor James Wuye and Imam Muhammad Ashafa."

41. Ibid.

42. "Imam Muhammad Ashafa and Pastor James Wuye, Laureates of the Foundation."

Trained teams from the (IMC) are frequently employed in conflict areas in order to mediate. Women are trained as mediators and appointed for intervention in conflicts. [The IMC has] developed a curriculum, which contributes to religious peace and is [used] in more than 30 schools in Northern Nigeria. [Furthermore] they have established peace camps with the goal of deconstructing [negative] enemy images with radical youths.[43]

In the last twenty years, the IMC, through their grassroots organization of over 10,000 members, has reached into the militias and trained them to become peace activists.[44]

Muhammad Ashafa and James Wuye themselves operate outside the safety and security of the center, to mediate between the parties in conflict all over Nigeria. Two of their many achievements are contributing to the reduction of conflicts in Kaduna in 2002 and in Yelwa in 2004. Due to the joint initiatives of Muhammad Ashafa and James Wuye, "a declaration of peace was signed, which was supported by various Christian and Muslim representatives. This declaration—the 'Kaduna Peace Declaration of Religious Leaders'—is today still seen as a model of religious peace in the north of Nigeria."[45]

When, in September 2005, "due to the release of Mohammed caricatures in the Danish daily *Jylland-Posten*, a regional conflict was impending in the north of Nigeria, Muhammad Ashafa and James Wuye interceded in the conflict as early as a few hours after the publication, by persuading Christian leaders to publicly condemn the caricatures. Thus a potential escalation with many deaths was avoided." The number of deaths that was avoided could have been considerable. In other Muslim countries riots erupted, many Christians were attacked, and more than 200 people were killed.[46]

With so much conflict in the world, Muhammad Ashafa and James Wuye are in much demand. Recently they have been involved training

---

Chirac Prize, http://www.fondationchirac.eu/en/2009/11/imam-muhammad-ashafa-and-pastor-james-wuye-laureates-of-the-fondation-chirac-prize/

43. Ibid.

44. Ibid.

45. "Hessian Peace Prize 2013 awarded to Imam Dr Muhammad Ashafa and Pastor Dr James Wuye." Online: http://www.hsfk.de/Newsdetail.25.0.html?tx_ttnews%5Btt_news%5D=1216&tx_ttnews%5BbackPid%5D=5&cHash=6ebfda773b&L=1

46. Ibid.

Muslims and Christians in interfaith conflict resolution, not only all over Nigeria, but also Kenya, Sudan (north and south), Burundi, Ghana, Sierra Leone, and Lebanon. And Muhammad and James "have since managed to spread their messages of conflict-resolution to all corners of the globe."[47]

The work of Muhammad Ashafa has meant he has been named as one of the "World's Most Influential Muslims," and the work he has done with James Wuye

> has earned them numerous accolades, including a "Heroes of Peace" Award from Burundi; the "Peace Activist Award" of the Tanenbaum Center of Interreligious Understanding; a joint "Honorary Doctorate" in Philosophy bestowed upon them in Kolkata, India; "Search for Common Ground on Interfaith Cooperation Award" USA; the "Bremen Peace Award" from the Threshold Foundation on interreligious reconciliation, and the "Hessian Peace Prize."[48]

Recently Imam Mohamed Magid wrote an open letter to all Muslims around the world, encouraging us to consider Muhammad Ashafa and James Wuye as true role models:

> In the Name of God The Most Gracious, Most Merciful
>
> Dear Fellow Brothers and Sisters in Islam,
>
> Horrific acts of violence demand from us Muslims and people of all faiths around the globe to stand up against all those who perpetrate such horrific acts. Violence of any kind against any people cannot be ignored. Transgressions against people's rights are occurring today across all boundaries. Regardless of what perpetrators of such acts claim to hold over any other person, to live safely is a right, and we must all stand up to protect the right for all people. *"Stand for justice even if it is against yourself."* (Qur'an *Surat-un-Nisa*, Chapter 4, Verse 135)
>
> It is those who truly know the religion of Islam who, despite our differences, engage in peaceful dialogue and wholeheartedly forsake acts of violence like this. As dedicate worshippers we recognize that an injustice in one part of the world is never validated by another injustice. Human life is sacred and it is never acceptable to take a person's life to promote a political agenda. Violence is never the answer. We must create a community of harmony with and respect for others.

---

47. Online: https://www.ashoka.org/fellow/mohammed-ashafa

48. Online: http://themuslim500.com/profile/imam-muhammad-ashafa

This is the example of our Prophet Muhammad (peace be upon him) and the teachings of our faith. In a time of our history, Muslims were persecuted to the point that they had to flee from their homes, and we must remember it was the gracious Christian King of Abyssinia who opened his arms, welcoming the Muslims to live safely in his land, under his protection. He helped us preserve the tradition of our Prophet and the peaceful and loving religion of Islam. Muslims must use the King's example in all of our interactions with people of other faiths. Umar ibn al-Khattāb, the second leader of the Muslim community after Prophet Muhammad's death (May God be pleased with him), out of respect for the Church decided not to pray in a Jerusalem Church so that Muslims would not incorrectly feel that they had any entitlement to take it over in the future. He taught us that it is the responsibility of Muslims to protect the religions and religious places of worship in lands in which Muslims are the majority or minority.

The beloved Prophet (peace be upon him) said, "Whoever violates the rights of the People of the Book, I will complain against them on the Day of Judgment." There is none amongst us who wants to be complained against by our Beloved Prophet and teacher. We share with you the words of our Beloved Prophet Muhammad Ibn Abdullah:

This is a message from Muhammad ibn Abdullah,
as a covenant to those who adopt Christianity,
near and far, we are with them.

Verily I, the servants, the helpers, and my followers
defend them,
because Christians are my citizens; and by God!
I hold out against anything that displeases them.

No compulsion is to be on them.
Neither are their judges to be removed from their jobs
nor their monks from their monasteries.

No one is to destroy a house of their religion,
to damage it, or to carry anything from it to the Muslims' houses.
Should anyone take any of these,
he would spoil God's covenant and disobey His Prophet.

Verily, they are my allies

and have my secure charter against all that they hate.
No one is to force them to travel or to oblige them to fight.
The Muslims are to fight for them.

If a female Christian is married to a Muslim,
it is not to take place without her approval.
She is not to be prevented from visiting her church to pray.

Their churches are to be respected.
They are neither to be prevented from repairing them
nor the sacredness of their covenants.

No one of the nation [Muslims] is to disobey the covenant
till the Last Day [end of the world].

We have the example of those before us, like the King of Abyssinia, and we have the example of those among us, like Pastor James Wuye and his friend, Imam Muhammad Ashafa. During violent clashes against each other in their days as youth in Nigeria, each suffered the loss of loved ones at the hands of the other. After years of being set on revenge the two were brought together and abandoned their hopes for revenge, opting instead for the hope of harmony and peace. Together, as friends of different faiths, they have established the Interfaith Mediation Center of the Muslim-Christian Dialogue Forum in Nigeria. Their courage and determination to rise above evil is what we must all strive toward. That is the teaching of all of our faiths, and the path to peaceful living.[49]

All of us who would engage in strong-but-gentle struggle for justice against injustice would do well to gather a group of friends, watch a DVD of the brilliant documentary *The Imam and The Pastor*, about Imam Ashafa and Pastor Wuye and their interfaith conflict resolution, and discuss what we can learn from their story for our struggle.

49. Magid, "Muslims Must Stand Up against the Horrific Attacks against Christians in Nigeria."

## Consider the inner dynamics of this *jihad*

1. *Emphasize spirit*—over and above politics.
2. *Practice prayer*—in the spirit of *Bismillah*.
3. *Listen to God*—declare *as-salam-o-alaikum*.
4. *Distrust labels*—go beyond the stereotypes.
5. *Take initiative*—move out of your comfort zone.
6. *Meet people*—get to know "others" face-to-face.
7. *Extend grace*—towards "friends" and "enemies."
8. *Have faith*—in the compassion of a common God.

## Consider the outer dynamics of this *jihad*

1. *Seek peace*—in every situation with everyone.
2. *Make contact*—by visiting with your "enemies."
3. *Express empathy*—care for them and their family.
4. *Increase connections*—ask them for a return visit.
5. *Nurture mutuality*—make "friends" with your "enemy."
6. *Honor friendship*—as the model for reconciliation.
7. *Create agency*—to train people in conflict-resolution.
8. *Release volunteers*—to mediate in conflict situations.
9. *Facilitate dialogue*—between Christians and Muslims.
10. *Negotiate agreements*—for formal peace settlements.

# Conclusion

## *Isa Jihad*

## The Kingdom of Heaven on Earth

The *Jihad* of Jesus is to the struggle to incarnate the kingdom of heaven on earth.

He says this "kingdom is not of this world."[1] It is not an imposed partisan political Christian or Islamic state, but a voluntary inclusive egalitarian spiritual community.

Jesus says, "my kingdom is not of this world, otherwise my supporters would fight," violently, like everyone else.[2] It is *in* the world, but not *of* the world.[3] It is not something we impose on others, but something we incarnate in our own life. In order for us to embody something of "heaven on earth," however partially and/or temporarily, Jesus tells us that we need to live out the Be-attitudes he advocated in the Beatitudes.

If we read the text carefully we see that both the first and the last Be-atitude are about experiencing the "kingdom of heaven," or what I call the *kingdom, ummah,* or *community of God.* And verse 5 seems to suggest those who inherit heaven, will do so on earth.

> 3 *Blessed are the poor in spirit,*
> *for theirs is the kingdom of heaven.*
> 4 *Blessed are those who mourn,*
> *for they will be comforted.*
> 5 *Blessed are the meek,*
> *for they will inherit the earth.*
> 6 *Blessed are those who hunger and thirst for righteousness,*

1. John 18:36
2. John 18:36
3. John 15:19

*for they will be filled.*
*7 Blessed are the merciful,*
*for they will be shown mercy.*
*8 Blessed are the pure in heart,*
*for they will see God.*
*9 Blessed are the peacemakers,*
*for they will be called children of God.*
*10 Blessed are those who are persecuted because of righteousness,*
*for theirs is the kingdom of heaven.*
MATTHEW 5:3–10

According to Jesus, in the Beatitudes, what Abbas al Aqqad calls the *Shari'ah of Isa*, the "kingdom of heaven," is a place where the meek inherit the earth (Matt 5:5); where those who give mercy will receive mercy (Matt 5:7); where the hungry will be filled (Luke 6:21), and those who hunger and thirst for justice will be fulfilled (Matt 5:6). It is a place where those who mourn will be comforted (Matt 5:4) and those who weep now will laugh once more (Luke 6:21). It is a place where peacemakers will walk proudly as sons and daughters of God (Matt 5:9), and all those who are pure in heart will see God (Matt 5:8).

This kingdom of heaven on earth—where people can see God face to face, live as God's children, be filled and fulfilled, find the comfort and the mercy that they need, wipe away their tears, and have a smile that no one can wipe off their face—it is the kind of place most of us hope and pray and deeply desire that our children's children would inherit.

## Being the Change We Want to See

However, Jesus says we are faced with a choice: to be—or not to be—the change we want to see. And in Luke's account of the beatitudes, Jesus makes the choice—and its consequences for us—painfully clear.

Looking at his disciples, he said:

*20 Blessed are you who are poor,*
*for yours is the kingdom of God.*
*21 Blessed are you who hunger now,*
*for you will be satisfied.*
*Blessed are you who weep now,*
*for you will laugh.*

²² *Blessed* are you when people hate you,

when they exclude you and insult you

and reject your name as evil,

because of the Son of Man.

²³ Rejoice in that day and leap for joy,

because great is your reward in heaven.

For that is how their ancestors treated the prophets.

²⁴ But *woe to* you who are rich,

for you have already received your comfort.

²⁵ *Woe* to you who are well fed now,

for you will go hungry.

*Woe* to you who laugh now,

for you will mourn and weep.

²⁶ *Woe* to you when all people speak well of you,

for that is how their ancestors treated the false prophets.

LUKE 6:20–26

In Luke's account of the beatitudes Jesus is using classic Jewish parallelism to compare and contrast two completely different positive and negative scenarios.

| Positive Scenario | Negative Scenario |
|---|---|
| Blessed are the poor (and those with the poor in spirit) for yours is the kingdom of God. | But woe to you who are rich, (and those into status/success) for you have received your comfort. |
| Blessed are you who hunger now, for you will be satisfied. | (But) woe to you who are well fed now, for you will go hungry. |
| Blessed are you who weep now, for you will laugh. | (But) woe to you who laugh now, for you will . . . weep. |
| Blessed are you when people hate you . . . because of the Son of Man, for that is how their ancestors treated the (true) prophets. | (But) woe to you when all people speak well of you, for that is how their ancestors treated the false prophets |

So Jesus is saying that we need to think about the consequences of our choices.

| Either we can . . . | Or we can . . . |
|---|---|
| Be poor<br>(or be with the poor in spirit)<br>And we will be blessed for the<br>   kingdom of God is ours. | Be rich<br>(and be into status and success)<br>And we will be cursed because we<br>   put our trust in riches. |
| Be hungry<br>(and hunger for justice),<br>and we will be blessed<br>for God will satisfy our hunger. | Be comfy<br>(and be well off and well fed),<br>and we will be cursed<br>for nothing will satisfy us. |
| Be sad,<br>(weeping with those who weep),<br>and we will be blessed for we will<br>   have the last laugh. | Be happy,<br>(laughing with those who laugh),<br>and we will be cursed for we will<br>   regret not really caring. |
| Be unpopular<br>(and get bad press)<br>because of our commitment<br>and we will be blessed because we<br>   are part of a great tradition of<br>   courageous integrity. | Be popular<br>(and get good press),<br>colluding with the status quo<br>and we will be cursed because we<br>   will have gained celebrity but<br>   lost our integrity in the process. |

Let us be frank, on first hearing the call to be poor, hungry, sad, and unpopular is not an attractive option, is it? It's exactly the opposite of what most of us aspire to.

But on second hearing, the call to be poor—to be with the poor in spirit; to be hungry—and to be hungry for justice; to be sad—because we are weeping with those that weep; and to be unpopular—because we are committed to follow the way of Christ with integrity—is quite intriguing, quite challenging, quite exciting.

And the more we think about it, the more we begin to slowly but surely realize that the call to be with the poor in spirit, to be hungry for justice, to be sad because we are weeping with those that weep, and to be unpopular because we are committed to follow the way of Christ with integrity, is in fact the only way that the kingdom of God can be ours, the only way that

God can satisfy our hunger for justice, and the only way that we can have the last laugh as part of that great tradition of people with integrity, who suffered scorn, but triumphed at the end. As my friend Brian McLaren says, "The kingdom of heaven comes to people who crave not victory but justice, who seek not revenge but mercy, who strive for peace and who are courageously eager to suffer pain for the cause of justice, not inflict it."[4]

And in the light of that knowledge we know we need to make a choice: *to be—or not to be—the change we want to see.*

If we want to be the change we want to see in the world, we need to practice to be:

| |
|---|
| poor—and/or identify with the poor in spirit |
| empathic—and grieve over the injustice in the world |
| meek—and get angry about injustice, but not aggressive |
| hungry and thirsty for righteousness—and seek for justice |
| merciful—and extend compassionate to all those in need |
| pure in heart—and whole-hearted in our desire to do right |
| peacemakers—and work for peace in a world that's at war |
| persecuted for righteousness—and suffer for just causes |

When I wanted to launch my *Plan Be* Series—three books I'd written on the Be-Attitudes as Jesus' framework for his nonviolent struggle for love and justice—I asked a Muslim friend, Nora Amath, the Director of AMARAH (Australian Muslim Advocates of the Rights of All Humanity) to introduce *Hey Be and See, Plan Be* and *See What I Mean* to a broad cross-section of a multi-faith community. And, these are excerpts from what she said:

> Peace and blessings be upon you all.
> I am honored to part of the launch of the Beatitudes books by my good friend Dave Andrews. When Dave asked me to say a few words about the series, I thought "Yep," I have heard Dave talk about the Beatitudes on a few occasions. "Easy." But when I read the books I couldn't put them down. I read them in two days straight. And it wasn't an easy two days. Don't get me wrong—the books were very well written, but they challenged me tremendously.

4. Mclaren, *Everything Must Change*, 177.

A few weeks ago I was part of a dialogue at a local church and someone asked if I was a Jesus–following Muslim. And I replied with an emphatic "Yes! of course I am. Every Muslim has to be. It is part of our belief. Yes, I and other Muslims believe that Jesus was here on Earth to convey and invite people to accept God's message. Thus we are followers of Jesus." But until I read Dave's books I really didn't know what that meant. Three books later, I do know what that line means—and I realize that I had a long way to go.

I think some of you may find all this quite ironic—a visible, devout Muslim (wearing a hijab) up here discussing a book written by a devout Christian about Jesus' Sermon on the Mount. But that, my friends, is the beauty of this series. I believe the Beatitudes is an ethical framework able to transcend all religious boundaries because its core, its essence, is part of every religious tradition. This radical, transformative framework is universal and can be applied within whichever religious tradition one comes from.

I thought long and hard about what it means to truly practice the Beatitudes, as a Muslim, [and] a servant of God. Using Dave's Be-Attitude framework:

I want to identify more with the poor "in spirit"

I want to grieve more over injustice in the world.

I can get angry, but vow never to get aggressive.

I seek to do and serve justice, even to my enemies.

I want to extend compassion to all those in need.

I want to act with integrity, not just for the publicity.

I would to work for peace in the midst of the violence.

And I would rather feel suffering myself, rather than inflict suffering.

I believe, actually, no, I know that once you finish [reflecting on] the Beatitudes you will realize your own capacity to make this world a better place. You will harness your faith in your Creator to serve by being part of this Be-Attitude revolution.

## The Good Samaritan/Christian/Muslim

Of all the tales Jesus tells, there is no better example of the embodiment of these Be-Attitudes than in the story of the man that we know of as the Good Samaritan.

> **25** On one occasion an expert in the law stood up to test Jesus. "Teacher," he asked, "what must I do to inherit eternal life?"
> **26** "What is written in the Law?" he replied. "How do you read it?"

27 He answered: "Love the Lord your God with all your heart and with all your soul and with all your strength and with all your mind; and, Love your neighbor as yourself." 28 "You have answered correctly," Jesus replied. "Do this and you will live." 29 But he wanted to justify himself, so he asked Jesus, "And who is my neighbor?" 30 In reply Jesus said: "A man was going down from Jerusalem to Jericho, when he fell into the hands of robbers. They stripped him of his clothes, beat him and went away, leaving him half dead. 31 A priest happened to be going down the same road, and when he saw the man, he passed by on the other side. 32 So too, a Levite, when he came to the place and saw him, passed by on the other side. 33 But a Samaritan, as he travelled, came where the man was; and when he saw him, he took pity on him. 34 He went to him and bandaged his wounds, pouring on oil and wine. Then he put the man on his own donkey, took him to an inn and took care of him. 35 The next day he took out two silver coins and gave them to the innkeeper. 'Look after him,' he said, 'and when I return, I will reimburse you for any extra expense you may have.' 36 Which of these three do you think was a neighbor to the man who fell into the hands of robbers?" 37 The expert in the law replied, "The one who had mercy on him." Jesus told him, "Go and do likewise."
(Luke 10:25–37)

Now what would you say is the point of this story?

I can think of three points.

The first point would be that *we need to extend compassion towards others.*

(Yes. But there is more)

The second point would be that *we need to extend compassion towards those who are not the same as us.*

(Yes. But if that was the only other point that Jesus wanted to make, the rescuer in the story would have been a Jew and the victim in the story would have been a Samaritan).

The third—and most important—point Jesus wanted to make in this story (by casting the Jew in the role of the victim and the Samaritan in the role of the rescuer) is that *sometimes the only way we are going to learn about the need to extend compassion towards those who are not the same as us is if we are taught it by a righteous person from a different religion.*

When we read the story of the Good Samaritan in the light of the Be-Attitudes we have discussed, it is clear that, on the one hand, Jesus was condemning the leaders of his own religion for not practicing what he preached; and on the other hand, was commending a despised person from a different religion as an great example of all that Jesus was on about.

The Good Samaritan embodied the Be-Attitudes perfectly. He identified with the *poor man* he came across *in spirit*. He *grieved* over the injustice done him like he *grieved* over the injustice done to himself. He got *angry enough to act*, but controlled his rage so he used his energy constructively to deal with the injustice. He *sought to do justice* to the victim, by rescuing him from danger, even though the Jew was the Samaritan's traditional enemy. He *extended mercy* to the broken man, by bathing his wounds in oil, binding his injuries in cloth, carrying him to safety on his donkey, and not only paying for his care at a roadside inn, but also offering to pay more, if what he had already paid was not enough. He *acted with integrity*, not for the publicity, by quietly helping the man, and then quickly moving on. In so doing he *built a bridge of peace* between the Samaritans and the Jews *at the risk of being ridiculed by both sides*. In other words, *the Good Samaritan beautifully embodied the Be-Attitudes celebrated in the Beatitudes*.

And Jesus says to all who would listen: "Go and do likewise" (Luke 10:25–37).

If Jesus was telling the story of the Good Samaritan to people today, I've no doubt he would give the role of the Good Samaritan to someone who is as much despised by us as Samaritans were despised by Jews in his day.

Who do you think Jesus would cast in the role of the Good Samaritan today?

I think it would depend on the prejudices of the person he was talking to. But my guess is there is a good chance that if Jesus were speaking to a Muslim, he would probably choose a Good Christian, like James Wuye, or Leymah Gbowee, for the role of the Good Samaritan, and if he were speaking to a Christian, he would probably choose a Good Muslim, like Muhammad Ashafa, or Malala Yousafzai, for the role of the Good Samaritan.

And Jesus says to all who would listen: "Go and do likewise."

# Afterword

Traditionally advocates of nonviolence do so on the basis of its *inherent virtue*. But we would do well to remember that virtue is considered valuable because it is *viable*—it is a way of working that is most likely to work well, for the welfare of all, over the long haul.

In their brilliant study on civil resistance, *Why Civil Resistance Works*, Erica Chenoweth and Maria Stephen, analyzed

> 323 historical examples of civil resistance campaigns that occurred over a span of more than one hundred years. Each case involved an intensive conflict, sometimes lasting several years, in which socio-political movements struggled to change regimes or gain major concessions from government adversaries. Comparing the results of violent and nonviolent methods, Chenoweth and Stephan show nonviolent methods are more effective than armed struggle. In the cases examined, nonviolent campaigns were successful 53 percent of the time, compared to a 26 percent success rate when violence was employed. Nonviolent methods were equally successful in democratic regimes and in repressive dictatorships.[1]

The analysis also shows that nonviolent forms of struggle are less likely to descend into civil war and "more likely to produce social and political changes that lead to freer and more democratic societies."[2]

David Cortright says of the book:

> Previously all studies of nonviolent action were based on cases studies or moral reasoning. This analysis shows that nonviolent action is not only the right thing to do morally but is also the most effective method politically. These findings fundamentally challenge traditional realist assumptions about the efficacy of military

---

1. Cortright, Review of *Why Civil Resistance Works*. Online: http://www.e-ir.info/2013/01/17/review-why-civil-resistance-works/

2 Ibid.

force and the nature of political power. The authors highlight the significance of political legitimacy and show that the withdrawal of social consent through mass civil disobedience can alter the relations of power. The result is one of the most important studies of nonviolent struggle since Gene Sharp's *The Politics of Nonviolent Action*.[3]

Much of the *Why Civil Resistance Works* is devoted to an analysis of the core factors of nonviolent action that are most responsible for political success. "The most important factor is what they call the 'participation advantage', the ability of nonviolent methods to mobilize massive numbers of people to participate in political struggle. Large campaigns are much more likely to succeed than small campaigns," they argue. As membership increases, so does the probability of success (p. 39). Mass participation "can erode a regime's main sources of power when the participants represent diverse sectors of society" (p. 30). Mass participation helps to explain why nonviolent movements are more likely to produce democratic outcomes. Nonviolent movements are by their very nature mass-based, participatory expressions of freewill. When the movements' leadership came to power, the foundations for democratic, representative government were already in place.[4]

In an armed struggle, by contrast,

the resistance is carried out by a smaller, specialized cadre of fighters. An armed insurgency must operate according to military discipline, and its success may depend on the isolation and impregnability of its command structure. In the heat of battle there is no room for debate or dissent. Armed movements are less able to accommodate factions and may turn on themselves in violent purges. Most of the armed revolutions of the twentieth century produced repressive and dictatorial regimes. Those who win by the gun tend to rule by the gun.[5]

Chenoweth and Stephan also identify the political dynamics that enable nonviolent movements to undermine the power of often heavily armed adversaries.

Nonviolent campaigns are better able than violent campaigns to withstand government repression. In 88 per cent of the cases

3. Ibid.
4. Ibid.
5. Ibid.

studied, opposition campaigns faced violent repression from their adversaries, but in many instances this repression was counter-productive and played to the advantage of the challengers. The violent repression of unarmed protest often creates a backfire effect, generating a sympathetic reaction among third parties that increases support for the protesters while undermining the legiti-macy and political support of the regime. Nonviolent movements are also more likely to induce loyalty shifts and defections among government officials and within the security forces. Through their analysis of the NAVCO data the authors observe that security force defections increase the probability of a campaign's success by 60 per cent" (p. 58).[6]

David Cortright says:

When resistance campaigns adopt a strategy of armed struggle they diminish their prospects for success and make it easier for the government to use force against them. When soldiers, civil servants, and third parties are attacked violently they tend to close ranks behind the regime and are less likely to shift their loyalties to the other side. Fear and anger within the population may prompt calls for retaliation and generate increased support for govern-ment repression. Officials who are under military attack tend to be less likely to negotiate and make political concessions.[7]

Chenoweth and Stephan's book:

breaks new ground in the study of nonviolent action and politi-cal science, but it also leaves much unsaid. The book pays scant attention to the role of political ideology, but it is obvious from the Iranian and Palestinian examples in the book, and the revolu-tion in Egypt, (militant) political Islam is a major factor driving popular mobilization and political outcomes—not always toward the democratic model.[8]

Which is why it is so important for Christians and Muslims to prac-tice the radical, alternative, participatory, empowering, nonviolent *jihad* of Jesus.

6. Ibid.
7. Ibid.
8. Ibid.

# Bibliography

Abaza, Ismail. "Baybars al-Bunduqdari: The First Great Slave Ruler of Egypt." Online: http://www.touregypt.net/featurestories/baybars.htm

Abi-Habib, Maria. "Iraq's Christian Minority Feels Militant Threat." *The Wall Street Journal*, 28 June 2014. Online: http://online.wsj.com/articles/iraqs-christian-minority-feels-militant-threat-1403826576

Adeyemo, Tokenboh. "Lessons from Rwanda." Paper delivered at Tear Australia Conference, 1996.

Agnihotri, V. K. *Indian History*. Mumbai: Allied, 2010.

Akcam, Taner. *a Shameful Act: The Armenian Genocide and the Question of Turkish Responsibility*. New York: Metropolitan, 2006.

Al-Ghazali. "The Sayings of Jesus." In *Al-Ghazali Ihya Ulum al-Din*, Book 4, Section 35. Karachi: Darul-Ishat, 1993.

Allport, Gordon, and Bernard Kramer. "Some Roots of Prejudice." *Journal of Psychology* 22 (1946) 9–39.

Al-Mahdy, Amin. "The Muslim Brotherhood and the Egyptian State in the Balance of Democracy." *Metransparent*. Online: http://www.metransparent.com/old/texts/amin_el_mahdi_the_muslim_brotherhood_and_the_egyptian_state.htm

Alpert, Richard. *Be Here Now*. New York: Crown, 1971

al-Salhy, Suadad. "Al Qaeda Tightens Grip on Western Iraq in Bid for Islamic State." Reuters. 11 December 2013. Online: http://www.reuters.com/article/2013/12/11/us-iraq-violence-al-qaeda-idUSBRE9BA0O820131211

Andrews, Dave. *Bismillah—A Christian-Muslim Ramadan Reflection*. Melbourne: Mosaic, 2012

———. *Building a Better World*. Sutherland, Australia: Albatross, 1996.

———. *Christi-Anarchy: Discovering a Radical Spirituality of Compassion*. Eugene, OR: Wipf and Stock, 2012.

———. *Hey, Be and See: We Can Be the Change You Want to See in the World*. Milton Keynes, UK: Authentic. 2009.

———. *Isa: A Christian-Muslim Ramadan Reflection*. Melbourne: Mosaic, 2013.

———. *Plan Be: Be the Change You Want to See in the World*. Milton Keynes, UK: Authentic. 2008.

———. *See What I Mean? See the Change We Can Be in the World*. Milton Keynes, UK: Authentic, 2009.

Arlandson, James. "A Brief Explanation of the Sword in Luke 22:36." Online: http://www.answering-islam.org/Authors/Arlandson/luke_22_36.htm

Armajani, Jon. *Modern Islamist Movements: History, Religion, and Politics*. New Jersey: Wiley-Blackwell, 2012.

Armstrong, Karen. *The Battle for God*. New York: Knopf, 2000.

Arnaz, Farouk. "Update: Explosion Was Suicide Attack, Indonesian Police Say." *The Jakarta Globe*, 15 April 2011. Online: http://thejakartaglobe.beritasatu.com/archive/suicide-bomber-praying-as-he-detonates-bomb-survivor/435595/

Ashafa, Muhammad. Online: https://www.ashoka.org/fellow/mohammed-ashafa

Aslan, Reza. *Zealot: The Life and Times of Jesus of Nazareth*. New York: Random House, 2013.

Astren, Fred. *Karaite Judaism and Historical Understanding*. Columbia: University of South Carolina Press, 2004.

Atwan, Abdel Bari. *The Secret History of Al Qaeda*. Oakland, CA: University of California Press, 2006.

Auron, Yair. *The Banality of Indifference: Zionism and the Armenian Genocide*. New Brunswick, NJ: Transaction, 2000.

Austin, Greg, et al. *God and War*. Bradford, UK: Department of Peace Studies, 2003.

Babur, *The Baburnama: Memoirs of Babur, Prince and Emperor*. Translated by Wheeler Thackston. Oxford: Oxford University Press, 1996.

Bakhash, Shaul. *Reign of the Ayatollahs*. New York: Basic, 1984.

Balakian, Peter. *The Burning Tigris: The Armenian Genocide and America's Response*. New York: HarperCollins, 2003.

Barclay, William. *Daily Study Bible*—Luke 6. Online: http://www.studylight.org/commentaries/dsb/view.cgi?bk=41&ch=6

———. *The Gospel of Luke*. Edinburgh: St. Andrew, 1975.

Barraclough, Ray. *Land Rights*. Brisbane: Student Christian Movement, 1988.

Beker, Avi. *The Chosen: The History of an Idea and the Anatomy of an Obsession*. New York: Palgrave McMillan, 2008.

Ben Sills, "Spanish Court to Deliver Verdict in Madrid Train Bombing Case." 31 October 2007. Online: http://www.bloomberg.com/apps/news?pid=newsarchive&sid=a6OX1U4VoJWM

Bencheikh, Soheib. "Islam and Secularism." In *Qantara.de*. Online: http://en.qantara.de/content/interview-with-soheib-bencheikh-islam-and-secularism

Bender, Jeremy. "Australia Is the Largest Per Capita Contributor of Foreign Fighters to ISIS." *Business Insider Australia*. 24 June 2014. Online: http://www.businessinsider.com.au/australia-is-major-contributor-of-isis-fighters-2014-6

Black, George. *Garrison Gautemala*. London: Zed, 1984.

Bloom, Jonathan, and Sheila Blair. "Islam—A Thousand Years of Faith and Power." Online: http://www.socialistworld.net/doc/245

Blum, William. "Great Moments in the History of Imperialism" Information Clearing House. 23 June 2006. Online: http://www.informationclearinghouse.info/article13719.htm

Bowker, John. "Al-Dajjal." In *Oxford Dictionary of World Religions*. Oxford: Oxford University Press, 1987.

Brinsmead, Robert. *The Two Sources of Morality and Religion*. New York: Henry Holt, 1989.

Broadbent, Edmund H. *The Pilgrim Church*. London: Pickering & Inglis, 1974.

Brown, Ian. *Khomeini's Forgotten Sons: The Story of Iran's Boy Soldiers*. London: Grey Seal, 1990.

Buck, Christopher. *Religious Myths and Visions of America*. Westport, CT: Praeger, 2009.

Budge, Ernest. *The Chronography of Bar Hebraeus*, Vol 1. Piscataway, NJ: Georgias, 2003.

Bulos, Nabih. "Islamic State of Iraq and Syria Aims to Recruit Westerners with Video." *LA Times.com*. 21 June 2014. Online: http://www.latimes.com/world/middleeast/la-fg-isis-video-20140620-story.html

Burke, Jason, and Paddy Allen. "The Five Ages of al-Qaida." *The Guardian*. 11 September 2009. Online: http://www.theguardian.com/world/interactive/2009/sep/10/al-qaida-five-ages-terror-attacks.

Buzan, Barry. *Regions and Powers*. Cambridge: Cambridge University Press, 2003.

Campbell, John. "Should U.S. Fear Boko Haram?" CNN 1 October 2010. Online: http://edition.cnn.com/2013/10/01/opinion/campbell-boko-haram/index.html.

Campbell, John. *Nigeria: Dancing on the Brink*. Lanham, MD: Rowman & Littlefield, 2013.

Canetti, Elias. *Crowds and Power*. London: Penguin, 1960.

Casper, Gretchen. *Fragile Democracies: The Legacies of Authoritarian Rule*. Pittsburgh, PA: University of Pittsburgh, 2009.

Chamieh, Jebran. *Traditionalists, Militants and Liberal in Present Islam*. Montreal: The Research and Publishing House, 1995.

Channer, Alan, producer/director. "The Imam and the Pastor Initiative of Change." London: FLT Films, 2006.

Chenoweth, Erica, and Maria J. Stephan. *Why Civil Resistance Works: The Strategic Logic of Nonviolent Conflict*. New York: Columbia University Press, 2011.

Chisholm, Hugh. "Constantinople, the Capital of the Turkish Empire." In *The Encyclopædia Britannica*. London: Encyclopædia Britannica, 1911.

Collins, J., "Rwanda." *Target* 4. (1994) 16.

Conde, Carlos H. "400 Killed by Terrorism in Philippines since 2000, Report Says." *The New York Times*, 30 July 2007. Online: http://www.nytimes.com/2007/07/30/world/asia/30iht-phils.4.6902202.htm

Cortright, David. Review of *Why Civil Resistance Works*, by Erica Chenoweth and Maria J. Stephan. Online: http://www.e-ir.info/2013/01/17/review-why-civil-resistance-works/

Coulton, G. G. *Inquisition and Liberty*. Gloucester, UK: Peter Smith, 1969.

Cragg, Kenneth. *Jesus and the Muslim: An Exploration*. Oxford: OneWorld, 1999.

Dadrian, Vahakn. *The History of the Armenian Genocide: Ethnic Conflict from the Balkans to Anatolia to the Caucasus*. Oxford: Berghahn, 1995.

Daniel-Rops, Henri, *Cathedral and Crusade*. New York: Dutton , 1957.

Delanoue, Gilbert. "al-Ik⬛h⬛wānal-Muslimūn." In *The Encyclopaedia of Islam*. Leiden: Brill. Online: http://www.brill.com/publications/online-resources/encyclopaedia-islam-online

Diamond, Sara. *Spiritual Warfare*. Boston: South End, 1989.

Dietl, Wilhelm. *Holy War*. New York: Macmillan, 1984.

Dixon, John. "How Reza Aslan's Jesus Is Giving History a Bad Name." Online: http://www.abc.net.au/religion/articles/2013/08/09/3822264.htm

Dominion, Jack. *Authority*. London: Darton, Longman & Todd, 1976.

Durand, Greg L. "Reconstructionism's Commitment to Mosaic Penology: Christian Reconstruction and Its Blueprints for Dominion." Online: http://en.wikipedia.org/wiki/Christian_Reconstructionism

Dyer, Gwynne. *War*. New York: Carroll & Graf , 2006.

Easwaran, Eknath. *A Man to Match His Mountains*. Petaluma, CA: Nilgiri, 1984.

Eikmeier, Dale. "Qutbism: An Ideology of Islamic-Fascism." *US Army War Quarterly*, Parameters (Spring 2007) 85–98.

Elegant, Simon. "Indonesia's Dirty Little Holy War." *Time.com*. 17 December 2001. Online: http://content.time.com/time/world/article/0,8599,187655,00.html

Ellerbe, Helen. *The Dark Side of Christian History*. San Rafael, CA: Morningstar, 1995.

Elliot, Henry M., and John Dowson. *The History of India, as Told by Its Own Historians. The Muhammadan Period, Vol. 1*. London: Trubner, 1867–77.

Elliott, Charles. *Comfortable Compassion*. London: Hodder and Stoughton, 1987.

Ellul, Jacques. *The Ethics of Freedom*. Grand Rapids: Eerdmans, 1967.

Esack, Farid. *Qur'an, Liberation and Pluralism*. Oxford: OneWorld, 1997.

Evans, Dominic, and Isra' al-Rube'l, "Convert, Pay Tax, or Die, Islamic State Warns Christians." *Huffington Post*, 19 July 2014. Online http://www.huffingtonpost.com/2014/07/19/islamic-state-christians-_n_5601839.html?utm_hp_ref=religion

Freud, Sigmund. *The Future of Illusion*. London: Hogarth, 1961.

Frey, Rebecca J. *Genocide and International Justice Global Issues*. New York: Infobase, 2009.

Gandhi, Mohandas. *The Message of Jesus*. Bombay: Bharitya Vidya Bhavan, 1971.

Gasiorowski, Mark J. "The Political Regimes Project." In *On Measuring Democracy: Its Consequences and Concomitants*, edited by Alex Inketes. New Bruswick: Transaction, 2006.

Gbowee, Leymah. *Mighty Be Our Powers*. New York: Best, 2011.

Gettleman, Jeffrey. "Sudanese Leader Mounts Charm Offensive." *NY Times.com*. 24 July 2008. Online: http://www.scribd.com/doc/190795929/NYPD-Westgate-Report#dow.

Glew-Crouch, Peter. *Religion and Helping Behaviour*. Hobart, Tasmania: University of Tasmania, 1989.

Goldhagen, Daniel J. *Hitler's Willing Executioners: Ordinary Germans and the Holocaust*. New York: Knopf, 1996.

Graham, Lloyd. *Deceptions and Myths of the Bible*. New York: Citadel, 1975.

Grossman, Dave. *On Killing*. New York: Back Bay, 2009.

Hafiz, Yasmina. "Sunni and Siite British Imams Denounce ISIS together in New Video." *Huffington Post*, 12 July 2014. Online: http://www.huffingtonpost.com/2014/07/12/imams-denounce-isis_n_5579370.html

Hallett, Robin. *Africa Since 1875*. Ann Arbor, MI: The University of Michigan Press, 1974.

Hambaryan, Azat S. *Hay Zhoghovrdi Patmut'yun 6*. Yerevan, Armenia: Armenian Academy of Sciences, 1981.

Hamlin, Rick. "Leymah Gbowee and the Hard Work of Faith." In *Guideposts*. Online: http://www.guideposts.org/blogs/journey/leymah-gbowee-and-hard-work-faith

Haught, James A. *Holy Horrors*. Buffalo, NY: Prometheus, 1990.

Hiebert, Paul. "Conversion, Culture, and Cognitive Categories." *Gospel in Context* 1.4 (1978) 24–29.

Hillgarth, N. J. *The Conversion of Western Europe*. Englewood Cliffs, NJ: Prentice Hall, 1969.

Hosein, Imran N. *Jerusalem in the Qur'an*. Long Island, NY: Masjid Dar al-Qur'an, 2002.

Hovannisian, Richard. *The Armenian Genocide: History, Politics, Ethics*. Basingstoke, UK: Palgrave, 1992.

Husain, Muhammad Kamel. *City of Wrong*. Amsterdam: Djambatan, 1958.

Inalcik, Halil. *The Ottoman Empire: The Classical Age 1300–1600*. London: Phoenix, 2000.

Jones, Stanley. *The Way*. London: Hodder & Stoughton, 1947.

Kamen, Henry. *Inquisition and Society in Spain*. Bloomington, IN: Indiana University Press, 1985.

Kelly, Jack. "Egypt's Muslim Brotherhood is Not to be Trusted." *Old Post-gazette*. 22 January 2012. Online: http://old.post-gazette.com/pg/12022/1204878–373–0.stm

Kelsey, Morton T. *The Other Side of Silence*. New York: Paulist, 1976.

Khalid, Khalid M. *Ma'an 'ala-l-Tariq: Muhammad wa-i-Masih*. Cairo: Dar alKutub al Haditha, 1958.

Khan, Maulana Wahiduddin. *The Prophet of Peace*. New Delhi: Penguin, 2009.

Kraybill, Donald. *The Upside Down Kingdom*. Scottdale, PA: Herald, 1978.

Kreider, Alan, and John H. Yoder. "Christians and War." In *The History of Christianity*, edited by Tim Dowley. Berkhamstead, UK: Lion, 1977.

Küng, Hans. *Christianity*. London: SCM, 1995.

Kuntzel, Matthias. "Ahmadinejad's Demons, a Child of the Revolution Takes Over." *The New Republic*, 24 April 2006. Online: http://www.matthiaskuentzel.de/contents/ahmadinejads-demons

Kurkjian, Vahan M. *A History of Armenia*. New York: The Armenian General Benevolent Union of America, 1958.

Lapidus, Ira M. *A History of Islamic Societies*. Cambridge: Cambridge University Press, 2002.

Latourette, Kenneth S. *A History of Christianity*, Vol. II. New York: Harper & Row, 1975.

Lea, Henry C. *The Inquisition of the Middle Ages*. New York: MacMillan, 1961.

Leonard, Tom. "Osama bin Laden Came within Minutes of Killing Bill Clinton." *The Daily Telegraph*, 25 December 2009. Online: http://www.telegraph.co.uk/news/worldnews/asia/philippines/6867331/Osama-bin-Laden-came-within-minutes-of-killing-Bill-Clinton.html

Levack, Brian P. *The Witch-Hunt in Early Modern Europe*. London: Longman, 1987.

Lewis, C. S. "The Inner Ring." C. S. Lewis Society of California. No pages. Online: http://www.lewissociety.org/innerring.php

Lincoln, Bruce. *Holy Terrors*. Chicago: University of Chicago Press, 2002.

Lindt, Andreas. "John Calvin." In *The History of Christianity*, edited by Tim Dowley. Berkhamstead, UK: Lion, 1977.

Mackey, Sandra. *The Iranians: Persia, Islam and the Soul of a Nation*. New York: Dutton, 1996.

Magid, Mohamed. "Muslims Must Stand Up against the Horrific Attacks against Christians in Nigeria." Online: http://www.huffingtonpost.com/imam-mohamed-magid/muslims-stand-up-against-nigeria-anti-christian-violence_b_1171584.html

Martin, Malachi. *Decline and Fall of the Roman Church*. New York: Putnam's Sons, 1981.

Marx, Karl. "Freedom of the Press." In *Selected Writings*, edited by David McLellan. Oxford: Oxford University Press, 1971.

Massoumi, Mejgan, and Nezar Al Sayyad. *The Fundamentalist City? Religiosity and the Remaking of Urban Space*. New York: Routledge, 2010.

McAlpine, Thomas. *Facing the Powers*. Monrovia, Liberia: MARC, 1991.

McCoy, Terrance. "ISIS, Beheadings and the Success of Horrifying Violence." *washingtonpost.com*. 13 June 2013. Online: http://www.washingtonpost.com/news/morning-mix/wp/2014/06/13/isis-beheadings-and-the-success-of-horrifying-violence/.

McGirk, Tim, and Shomali Plain. "Lifting the Veil on Taliban Sex Slavery." *Time*, 10 February 2002. Online: http://content.time.com/time/magazine/article/0,9171, 201892,00.html .

Mclaren, Brian. *Everything Must Change*. Nashville: Thomas Nelson, 2007.

Milgram, Stanley. "The Perils of Obedience." *Harper's Magazine* (1974). Online: http:// www.age-of-the-sage.org/psychology/milgram_perils_authority_1974.html

———. *Obedience to Authority: An Experimental View*. London: Tavistock, 1974.

Mir, Hamid. "Osama Claims He Has Nukes: If U.S. Uses N-arms It Will Get the Same Response." *Dawn: the Internet Edition*, 10 November 2001. Online: http://www. oocities.org/stopamerica/articles/dawnvw.html

Moin, Baqer. *Khomeini: Life of the Ayatollah*. New York: Dunne, 2000.

Mooney, Mick. "The Problem with Interpreting Jesus' Words Literally." Online: http:// mickmooney.com/literal-interpretation/

Morgan, Diane. *Essential Islam: a Comprehensive Guide to Belief and Practice*. Santa Barbara: ABC-CLIO, 2010.

Morgenthau, Henry. *Ambassador Morgenthau's Story*. New York: Doubleday, 1918.

Muir, William. *The Caliphate: Its Rise, Decline, and Fall from Original Sources*. Whitefish, MT: Kessinger, 2004.

Mulligan, Hugh A. "Columbus Saga Sinking Fast." Associated Press, 8 March 1992.

Murray, Micah J. "The God Who Bleeds" In *Redemption Pictures*. Online: http:// redemptionpictures.com/2013/10/23/the-god-who-bleeds/#sthash.oId4sOQq.dpuf

Neill, Stephen. *A History of Christian Missions*. Harmondsworth, UK: Penguin, 1975.

Nigg, Walter. *The Heretics: Heresy through the Ages*. New York: Dorset, 1962.

Pagels, Elaine. *Adam, Eve and the Serpent*. New York: Random House, 1988.

Palmer, J. A. B. "The Origin of Janissaries." *Bulletin of the John Rylands Library* 35.1 (1952) 448–51.

Panati, Charles. *Panati's Extraordinary Endings of Practically Everything*. New York: Harper & Row, 1989.

Peck, M. Scott. *The People of The Lie*, Melbourne: Rider Books, 1983.

Pensar, Jed. "A Critique of Islamic Jihad." Online: http://www.krim.org/links/A_Critique_ of_Islamic_Jihad2.htm

Peretti, Frank. *Piercing The Darkness*. Westchester, NY: Crossway, 1988.

———. *This Present Darkness*. Westchester, NY: Crossway, 1986.

Plaidy, Jean. *The Spanish Inquisition*. New York: Citadel, 1967.

Qutb, Sayyid. *Milestones*. Chicago: Kazi, 2003.

Radwan, Zahra, and Zoe Blumenfeld. "Surging Violence against Women in Iraq." In Inter Press Service. 27 June 2014. Online: http://www.ipsnews.net/2014/06/op-ed-surging-violence-against-women-in-iraq/

Ramsay, W. M. *Impressions of Turkey during Twelve Years' Wanderings*. London: Hodder and Stoughton, 1897.

Rane, Halim. *Reconstructing Jihad amid Competing International Norms*. New York: Palgrave Macmillan, 2009.

Robbins, Rossell H. *The Encyclopaedia of Witchcraft and Demonology*. New York: Bonanza, 1981.

Robinson, H. Wheeler. *Christian Doctrine of Man*. Edinburgh: T. & T. Clark, 1913.

Rokeach, Milton. *The Open and Closed Mind*. New York: Basic, 1960.

Roshandil, Jalil, and Chadha Sharon. *Jihad and International Security*. New York: Macmillan, 2006.

Roth, Cecil. *The Spanish Inquisition*. New York: Norton, 1964.

Runciman, Steven. *A History of The Crusades*, Vol 1. Cambridge: Cambridge University Press, 1951.

Russell, Jeffrey B. *A History of Medieval Christianity*. New York: Crowell, 1968.

Sardar, Ziauddin. "Rethinking Islam." In *Islam for Today*. June 2002. Online: http://islamfortoday.com.sardar01.htm

Satha-Anand, Chaiwat. "The Nonviolent Crescent." In *Islam and Nonviolence*, edited by Glenn D. Paige et al. Honolulu: Center For Global Nonviolence Planning Project, 1993.

Saul, John Ralston. *The Unconscious Civilization*. New York: Simon & Schuster, 1995.

Schaff, Philip. *History of The Christian Church*, Vol. V. Grand Rapids: Eerdmans, 1952.

Schirazi, Asghar. *The Constitution of Iran*. London: Tauris, 1997.

Sebeos. *The Armenian History attributed to Sebeos*. Translated by R. W. Thomson. Liverpool: Liverpool University Press, 1999.

Sharp, Gene. *Power and Struggle*. Boston: Sargent, 1973.

Shawqi, Ahmand. *Al-Shawqiyyat*, Vol. 2. Beirut: Dar al-'Awah, 1988.

Silinsky, Mark. *Jihad's Charisma: Mullah Omar, Osama bin Laden and Charismatic Leadership in Afghanistan*. London: Association for the Study of Ethnicity and Nationalities, London School of Economics, 2010. Online: http://www.lse.ac.uk/researchAndExpertise/units/ASEN/Conference/PastConferences/2010/conferencepapers2010/Mark_Slinsky

Simone, Samira. " Feared Basij Militia Has Deep History in Iranian Conflict." CNN. 22 June 2009. Online: http://edition.cnn.com/2009/WORLD/meast/06/22/iran.basij.militia.profile/index.html

Singer, Peter W. *Children at War*. Berkeley, CA: University of California Press, 2006.

Sly, Liz. "Al-Qaeda Disavows Any Ties with Radical Islamist ISIS group in Syria, Iraq." *The Washington Post*, 3 February 2014. Online: http://www.washingtonpost.com/world/middle_east/al-qaeda-disavows-any-ties-with-radical-islamist-isis-group-in-syria-iraq/2014/02/03/2c9afc3a-8cef-11e3-98ab-fe5228217bd1_story.html.

Smith, Charles Merrill. *The Pearly Gates Syndicate*. New York: Doubleday, 1971.

Smith, John Holland. *The Death of Classical Paganism*. New York: Scribner, 1976.

Sookhdeo, Patrick. *Global Jihad: The Future in the Face of Militant Islam*. McLean, VA: Isaac, 2007.

Spencer, Richard. "Iraq Crisis: UN Condemns 'War Crimes' as Another Town Falls to Isis." *The Telegraph*, 16 June 2014. Online: http://www.telegraph.co.uk/news/worldnews/middleeast/iraq/10904414/Iraq-crisis-UN-condemns-war-crimes-as-another-town-falls-to-Isis.html.

Stassen, Glen, and David Gushee. *Kingdom Ethics*. Downers Grove, IL: IVP, 2003.

Stellaway, Richard. "Religion." In *Christian Perspectives in Sociology*, edited by Stephen A. Grunlan and Milton Reimer. Grand Rapids: Zondervan, 1982.

Steward, John. "Rwanda Report." Email from Australian practitioner to the author about his work in Rwanda, 1997.

Stewart, Catrina. "Illegal Ivory Trade Funds al-Shabaab's Terrorist Attacks." *The Independent*, 6 October 2013. Online: http://www.independent.co.uk/news/world/africa/illegal-ivory-trade-funds-alshabaabs-terrorist-attacks-8861315.html.

Stouffer, Samuel. *Communism, Conformity and Civil Liberties*. Garden City, NY: Doubleday, 1955.

Stupperich, Robert. "Martin Luther." In *The History of Christianity*, edited by Tim Dowley. Berkhamstead, UK: Lion, 1977.

"The Taliban's War on Women." Physicians for Human Rights, August 1998. Online: https://www.law.georgetown.edu/rossrights/docs/reports/taliban.pdf.

Thomas, Keith. *Religion and the Decline of Magic*. London: Penguin, 1971.

Tibi, Basam. *Islam between Culture and Politics*. Basingstoke, UK: Palgrave Macmillan, 2005.

Tompkins, Peter. *The Magic of Obelisks*. New York: Harper, 1981.

Toynvbee, Arnold. British Foreign Office 371/2781/264888, Appendices B. Kew, UK: British Foreign Office Archives, 6.

Troll, Christian. "The Qur'anic View of Other Religions: Grounds for Living Together." *Islam and the Modern Age* 18.1 (1987) 5–19.

Tuchman, Barbara. *A Distant Mirror*. New York: Ballantine, 1978.

Vryonis, Seporos Jr. *Stanford J. Shaw, History of the Ottoman Empire and Modern Turkey, Vol 1, Empire of the Gazis, the Rise and Decline of the Ottoman Empire: A Critical Analysis*. Thessaloniki: Institute for Balkan Studies, 1983.

Walker, Andrew. "What is Boko Haram?" US Institute of Peace. June 2012. Online: http://www.usip.org/sites/default/files/resources/SR308.pdf .

Walker, Barbara G. *The Woman's Dictionary of Myths and Secrets*. San Francisco: Harper & Row, 1969.

Walker, Christopher. *Armenia: The Survival of a Nation*. London: Croom Helm, 1980.

Webbe, Gale. *The Night and Nothing*. New York: Seabury, 1964.

Weber, Max. *The Theory of Social and Economic Organisations*. Glencoe, IL: Free, 1947.

Whinfield, Edward Henry. *Masnavi-i-Ma'navi: Spiritual Couplets*. London: Trubner, 1887.

Wink, Walter. *Engaging the Powers: Discernment and Resistance in a World of Domination*. Minneapolis: Fortress, 1992.

———. *The Human Being: Jesus and the Enigma of the Son of the Man*. Minneapolis: Fortress, 2001.

Withey, Andree, and Leonie Mellor. "Brisbane Mosque Service Brings Christian and Muslim Leaders Together." ABC News. Online: http://www.abc.net.au/news/2014-09-26/interfaith-service-at-kuraby-mosque-christians-muslims/5771034?&section=news

Withnall, Adam. "Iraq Crisis: Isis Changes Name and Declares Its Territories a New Islamic State with 'Restoration of Caliphate' in Middle East." *The Independent*. 29 June 2014. Online: http://www.independent.co.uk/news/world/middle-east/isis-declares-new-islamic-state-in-middle-east-with-abu-bakr-albaghdadi-as-emir-removing-iraq-and-syria-from-its-name-9571374.html

Wright, Derek. *Psychology and Moral Behaviour*. Baltimore: Penguin, 1971.

Wright, Lawrence. *The Looming Tower: Al-Qaeda and the Road to 9/11*. New York: Knopf, 2006.

Wright, Robin. *The Last Great Revolution: Turmoil and Transformation in Iran*. New York: Knopf, 2000.

Yar-Shater, Ehsan. "The Crisis of the Early Caliphate." In *The History of al-Tahari*, Vol XV, translated and annotated by R. Stephen Humphreys. New York: State University of New York Press, 1993.

York, Kevin. "Analysis of al-Shabaab's Attack at the Westgate Mall in Nairobi, Kenya." New York Police Department. Online: http://www.scribd.com/doc/190795929/NYPD-Westgate-Report#dow.

Zaeef, Abdul Salam. "Taliban Spokesman: Cruel Behavior was Necessary." Tolonews.com. December 31, 2011. Online: https://www.youtube.com/all_comments?threaded=1&v=XAJwI-7KWlk.

Zimbardo, Philip. *The Lucifer Effect*. London: Rider, 2009.

Lightning Source UK Ltd.
Milton Keynes UK
UKOW06f2319121015

260410UK00001B/103/P